THE FARMER'S WIFE GUIDE TO GUIDE TO FABULOUS FRUITS AND BERRIES

THE FARMER'S WIFE GUIDE TO FABULOUS FRUITS AND BERRIES

GROWING, STORING, FREEZING,
AND COOKING YOUR OWN
200+ RECIPES
AND SERVING IDEAS!

WRITTEN AND ILLUSTRATED BY

Barbara Doyen

M. EVANS AND COMPANY, INC.
NEW YORK

M. Evans and Company, Inc.
216 East 49th Street
New York, New York 10017

Library of Congress Cataloging-in-Publication Data

Doyen, Barbara.
    The farmer's wife guide to fabulous fruits and berries : growing, storing, freezing, and cooking your own / by Barbara Doyen.
        p. cm.
    Includes bibliographical references (p.).
    ISBN 0-87131-975-6
    1. Fruit-culture. 2. Fruit. 3. Berries. 5. Cookery (Berries) I. Title: Fabulous Fruits and berries. II. Title.
SB355.D77 2002
634—dc21   2002020244

Book design by Rik Lain Schell

Printed in the United States of America

9 8 7 6 5 4 3 2 1

Contents

*To my husband, The Farmer (also known as Bob Doyen),
who talked me into becoming The Farmer's Wife.*

**"THE WEALTH OF MAN STARTS WITH
FOOD PRODUCED FROM THE SOIL."**

—Arnie Waldstein

WHY RAISE FRUITS AND BERRIES?

In the old days, farm folk had to be self-sufficient. When times were tough, the only fruit you might have was what you could raise yourself. Today, fruit is available in abundance, nearly year-round. So why raise your own?

It's Satisfying

There is something wonderful about stepping out your back door to pick crisp, juicy apples off your very own tree or tangy-sweet raspberries off bushes planted with your own hands, to serve fresh for supper. Or to make your own homegrown fruits and berries into flavorful pies or ice cream to share with friends as you sit and visit on your patio under a grape or kiwi arbor.

Home-Raised Fruit Tastes Better

You can harvest it at just the right time, at the peak of flavor. Store-bought fruit is often harvested unripe because it ships better that way. Sometimes fruit is altered by processing: for instance, it might be gassed to induce ripeness. Or waxed to prevent moisture loss. Or dyed to look prettier. Your own fruit is the real thing, wholesome in its natural goodness, the way nature intended.

You Can Grow Exactly the Varieties You Desire

For each fruit type, there are several choices that would be appropriate for your growing conditions. Each one has different attributes and a different flavor—you select what is right for you. Sometimes, the variety you prefer is not available in the store, like the Wealthy apples that were my Grandpa Hartsock's favorite, so I have planted a tree in my orchard in his memory.

Nutrition Is Improved

Did you know that strawberries picked on a sunny day have lots more vitamin C than those harvested on a cloudy day? Beyond this, shipping delays, premature harvest, and processing techniques rob the fruit of valuable nutrients.

You Have Control of the Pesticides You're Consuming

Fruit, especially when imported from other countries, may have been sprayed with toxic chemicals. By growing your own, you will know exactly what was used on your fruit, and since you have many choices, why not select products that work in cooperation with nature and are not harmful to our bodies?

Your Home and Yard Are Beautified

Fruited plants provide a landscape that is ever-changing from spring through fall and even into the winter. Your fruit trees, shrubs, vines, and plants will be pleasing from the eagerly awaited first budding in the spring, through the spectacular beauty of full blossoming, to the bright flashes of developing fruit, and even past the harvest when the foliage goes into fall color. The bare branches will add stark accents to your winter landscape as they throw soft shadows from the weaker winter sun; become painted with frost on a crisp, cool morning; or as they are quietly coated with the first snow on a gray November day.

Growing Your Own Fruit Is Easy!

Once established, it takes little time and minimal effort for great rewards!

It's Good for Your Mental, Spiritual, and Physical Well-Being

Raising your own fruits and berries presents you with a built-in opportunity to turn your attention away from your hectic day-to-day existence and tune in to the calming infinity of nature. Just as the fruit is connected and in harmony to the earth via roots and leaves and vital energy, you'll discover yourself becoming deeply connected and in harmony, too. This connection is not only mental and spiritual, but I believe it to be physical as well. The produce you raise likely has properties that help your body prepare for the conditions of the season to come via the same mechanism that triggers the woolly caterpillars to grow more hair, or wild animals to have thicker pelts and dig deeper holes for hibernation in anticipation of a harsher-than-normal winter. Perhaps eating locally grown fruit is important for your body's preparation for whatever the next season will bring.

I hope this book inspires you to grow fruits and berries, no matter what your situation. You'll look forward to walking around outside to observe and tend your crops or to caring for your indoor container plants. You'll find yourself reaping a dual harvest: wholesome fruits and berries for your body, and, as a bonus, nourishing fruits of the spirit for your soul.

GARDEN NOTES

Where to Find Space for Growing Fruits and Berries

Although my farm home is situated on a twelve-acre yard, and I have plenty of space for an orchard, if this farmer's wife were to move to town, you can bet my landscape would soon include fruiting trees, shrubs, and plants.

Even if my house had no outdoor garden area, I'd manage to raise fruit trees, bushes, or plants in containers, indoors or on a balcony outside. It can be done. I started my eight-foot-tall lemon tree from seed in my living room, and it's even produced lemons, an impossible feat outdoors because of our cold winters. A friend started a bush cherry in her apartment living room, and it actually produces delicious cherries year after year! Single-stem apple trees or espaliered dwarfs grow well in containers, take up little space on tiny balconies, and can even be underplanted with strawberries.

Most people will want to grow fruit outdoors, so that will be the main focus of this book. And most people live in town, not on a farm with ample room to grow as much as they desire. So how can you find space for fruit without a generous yard?

Here are some ideas:

VINES. Grape and kiwi are very attractive and can be trained to grow on a fence or wall or perhaps on an ornamental arch or arbor.

Or, they can form a shady patio roof, lending architectural interest to the landscape as well as edible fruit.

SHRUBS. Instead of considering traditional shrubs for foundation planting, why not think fruitfully? Elderberries make a lovely specimen shrub all year round, and gooseberries can be used as a foundation planting. Fruit bushes can be used for specimen planting, to line a pathway, or as a hedge that happens to bloom as well as provide food and colorful fall foliage. Consider blackberries, blueberries, raspberries, elderberries, bush cherries, or bush apricots.

TREES. For a lovely show of spring blossoms, summer shade, and to enhance your landscape design as well as provide a bountiful harvest, consider fruit trees. If you have a small yard, you can plant the dwarf variety. If space is really limited, try one of the pole apple varieties that grow only eight feet tall and two feet wide and are really only a trunk without branches. Or consider espalier, training a tree to grow flat against a wall—it's fun and lovely! Fruit trees can be shaped in all sorts of interesting ways. How about growing a living gazebo from apple trees planted in a circle and trained to shape a roof? Or a living fence of espaliered fruit trees trained to grow together into a solid lattice wall like a row of interconnected fans? Besides apple, other fruiting trees include apricot, cherry, mulberry, peach, nectarine, pear, and plum.

PLANTS. Rhubarb is an attractive perennial that grows two or three feet tall and has large tropical-looking leaves that look great with flowers or against a wall or fence. Watermelon and cantaloupe plants are available in compact forms that fits well into the landscape if you don't have room for the sprawling vine types. If you can't afford the space for a separate patch, why not use strawberries to edge flowerbeds or in landscaped berms? You can build a pyramid planter that allows you to grow lots of strawberries in a minimum of space. Or use strawberry pots, which are tall containers with plant openings along the outer wall for growing a lot of fruit, even on a deck or patio.

Location

FIRST, CHECK YOUR TOPOGRAPHY

A true farmer always evaluates the lay of the land before planting anything. Things to consider:

LOW SPOTS. Avoid planting fruits in low areas if you live in climates prone to frost during flowering or harvesting seasons. The colder air, being heavier than warm air, settles in low areas. Study where the early morning frost accumulates on your property—the densest patches are the cold spots. Low spots also collect water, which can drown plants. Our low farmland produces a bumper crop, but it survives to be harvested only one out of four years.

HILLS. During winter, the top of a hill could experience bitter, cold winds. In summer, there could be drying winds.

SLOPE. If you are raising fruit that might be damaged by spring frost, try to plant it on land that slopes to the east (ideal) or to the south (almost ideal). The reason? The night temperature is usually coldest right before the sun rises, so situate the more vulnerable fruit trees, shrubs, or plants so that they can capture the earliest sun for warmth. If the fruit slopes to the west, it will have to suffer the frost longer until the sun has risen high enough to reach it.

DRAINAGE. Avoid planting fruit in areas prone to standing water, or find a way to eliminate the water problem by installing a drainage system or raising the ground level. Soggy soil doesn't allow the roots to breathe. Low farmland gets used for pasture ground, especially if it's been tiled for drainage, but farmers also provide a hill for the livestock to retreat to in case of flooding.

WINDBREAKS. Traditionally, farmers planted rows of trees to break the strong winter winds, but a hedge, a building, or even a fence can also serve as a windbreak. When we were starting our orchard, we put up a new grove of pine trees as well as a lilac hedge

12

to protect the fruit trees. A living windbreak requires planning—you want it far enough away that the roots aren't in competition, yet close enough to serve the purpose. Generally, a windbreak protects for a distance of five times its height on the downwind side. Give thought to windbreak placement and the effect on snow drifts, because snow will accumulate on the downwind side. This would not be a good thing if it dumps huge piles of snow on your driveway, for instance. Or on your house.

STREET LIGHTS OR SPORTS FIELD LIGHTS. If they are bright, they might affect the hardiness of plants and trees planted nearby, because the plants and trees perceive the days as longer and they don't prepare for winter.

SALT. Ice-melting products used on roads or sidewalks can kill plants and trees. Last winter, these products also ruined our sidewalk.

A LAKE, OCEAN, OR OTHER LARGE BODY OF WATER. These can affect the climate on nearby land; the temperature can become less cold in the winter or less hot in the summer. It can also mean constant winds.

WELLS AND OTHER OBSTACLES. Be thoughtful about planting large trees near a well, as the roots could interfere with or damage the well. You should also avoid water or sewer lines and underground power, gas, and phone lines.

CONSIDER THE SOIL

What's a farmer's single most important asset? Dirt! With good dirt (and sunlight and water), you can grow anything; without good dirt, nothing will grow. It all begins with the soil.

If you aren't blessed with wonderful dirt, don't despair. Almost any soil can be made suitable with a little effort.

Is your soil mostly sand? Add a lot of compost—organic material that decomposes into soil. Lay down at least six inches of well-rotted manure and/or compost onto the planting area and till it into the sand, preferably a few months before you want to plant.

Is your soil mostly clay? Again, well-rotted manure and/or compost is the answer. Wait until the clay is partly dry to till in the compost because it's difficult to do when it's greasy. If the clay is really heavy and holds water, you might want to add a little sand to the mixture—this will help with drainage.

Does your soil lack fertility? Think well-rotted manure and/or compost.

Even if your soil is wonderful loam, compost will benefit it by adding nutrients and aerating the soil. It also makes the soil attractive to earthworms, and earthworms make the soil light and airy as they tunnel, and their castings add nutrients.

Think about what was growing in the soil in the preceding year or two. In general, it's best that you do not locate fruit trees on ground where roses, potatoes, tomatoes, eggplant, or peppers grew recently. They can pick up fungal diseases, even if the previous plant material showed no signs of them.

FEEDING

MANURE. I much prefer this natural "organic" type of fertilizer. There is nothing better than good old well-rotted hog, cattle, or chicken manure to produce a bountiful crop! For new planting, just mix it in with the planting soil. For existing plants, trees, or shrubs, just spread a layer one or two inches deep as far out as the plant is wide, in the early spring. If it won't damage the roots, you can lightly till the manure into the surface of the soil, or else just leave it on top, perhaps covered by mulch. It's hard to go wrong using manure, so long as it's properly aged. Using fresh manure near plants will burn them, often even killing them.

NOTE: Do not use pet or human waste as fertilizer for food crops. These can be dangerous unless properly handled.

If you don't have a source for manure, you can buy fertilizers at your local nurseries or from catalogues. You might consider the fertilizers in the Gardens Alive! catalogue (see "Sources"), which are natural and formulated to specific crops.

CHEMICAL FERTILIZERS. These are rapid acting and you must be careful not to use too much or to apply them at the wrong times. For instance, you should never use chemical fertilizers in the fall, because it will stimulate the plant to grow just when it should be shutting down in preparation for winter dormancy. A chemical fertilizer at this time will jeopardize the plant's winter survival. Always follow the product instructions carefully.

COMPOST. This is a good alternative to manure. Like manure, compost breaks down slowly, providing the plant a steady source of nutrition as it enriches the soil, and it's hard to go wrong with it. It's also readily available. Compost might be the only fertilizer you'll need.

Where to Get Compost

MAKING YOUR OWN. Farmers' wives call them pig buckets, and we keep them in the cabinet under the kitchen sink. Any throwaway plant material like potato or apple peelings, the outer leaves of cabbage and lettuce, overripe peaches—all this gets placed in the pig bucket. Hogs love the plant material, so when we had hogs, over the fence it went. Now we compost it!

But doesn't the compost bucket create an unpleasant odor in the kitchen? you ask. Not at all! Just remember one rule: Never add animal or dairy products to the pig bucket because you risk breeding dangerous bacteria, and your bucket—and house—will smell bad.

When the bucket is full, just haul it outside—daily in the summer, perhaps weekly in the winter. To make compost, we just dump the pig bucket material on the ground at the edge of a field, along with any plant debris from the garden or yard, like weeds, leaves, and so forth. Contact with the earth along with an occasional light tilling and a little rain soon reduces the plant material to compost. The compost pile doesn't have a bad odor, either—it just smells like the earth, which is what it's becoming. Since it's unsightly, locate your compost pile someplace where it will be blocked from view, say, behind a storage shed, or even screened by plants. Or consider buying a special compost bin that tidies up the appearance and speeds up the composting process. You'll probably want two chambers—one to be processing a batch and the other to collect plant material for the next batch.

About grass clippings: We don't use lawn chemicals, but if you do, you might want to avoid adding the grass clippings to your compost pile.

OTHER SOURCES OF COMPOST. Many areas have community compost piles. Material like plant debris and leaves are collected instead of burned or buried, and made into compost, which gardeners can load up and take home.

How to Use Compost

It's simple. Once it's "ripe," that is, the pile has deteriorated into a crumbly material that looks like coarse earth, just scoop it into a five-gallon bucket or small wheelbarrow and spread it around beneath your fruits and berries at any time. You can also mix it into the soil at planting time.

MOISTURE

With only a few exceptions, when you are watering fruits or berries, do not water lightly. It's far better to water deeply and less often than to water shallowly and more frequently.

Having soil that drains well is most important. Most roots hate to be in soggy soil, or, even worse, standing water. To allow for drainage, you can till sand into your soil, or plant in a raised bed or berm, or on a slope so that the excess water will run off.

Another way to eliminate standing water is to install drainage tiles, which make soggy soil plantable. Every farmer knows about this, because without tiling, excess water would accumulate and we'd never have crops. Even with tiling, flooding occurs when we have excessive rains.

If you don't get at least one inch of rain per week, you will have to water your newly planted fruits and berries, at least for the first year. Most need ample water during blooming and fruit development. Newly planted trees should receive at least five gallons of water per week from the time they're planted until the ground freezes. The soil should be moist to a depth of at least twelve inches.

A local tree professional tells me that the main reason trees don't survive their first winter is that they get too dry. He tells his customers that the best thing you can do is enjoy your Thanksgiving dinner and then go out and generously water your trees and shrubs to give them one last good drink before winter. Even dormant plants bring moisture up through their roots, which gets evaporated in the wind, and if there isn't enough moisture available, the roots eventually dry up, killing the plant.

On the other hand, too much water—soggy soil or standing water—can drown a plant because the water takes the place of air in the soil and the roots can't breathe. Plants differ in their tolerance of moisture, and this is detailed in the listings.

Drip irrigation is the best method, because the moisture is directed at the roots. If you must use overhead spraying, try to do it early in the morning on a sunny day so that the plants dry quickly, to prevent disease problems.

The best water is untreated. Fortunately, we have our own well. Some gardeners without wells choose to collect rainwater from their roofs and gather it in barrels. Some cities sell untreated water at the water plant, but you must have a tank and the means to haul it home.

Selecting Fruits

Farmers are very particular in choosing what they plant; the survival of their farming operation might depend on it. With so many fruiting varieties available, there are bound to be some that will work well in your particular area and others that will not. Things to consider:

YOUR CLIMATE. Select only those fruits that are suitable for your growing area. That way, you won't plant a tree that can withstand winter temperatures of only twenty degrees above zero when your winters get down to twenty degrees below zero—it's a sure bet that tree won't be alive the following spring!

To match a particular fruit variety to your climate, consult your local nursery or extension office or read the nursery catalogues that arrive in abundance during the winter. The catalogues often include a hardiness map and each fruit listing will include hardiness information and the range of recommended planting zones. To learn what zone you live in, consult a hardiness map or ask for information at your local nursery or extension office.

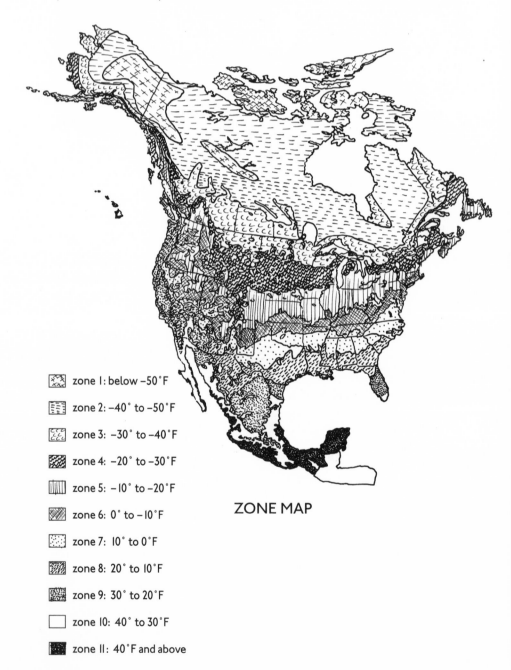

zone 1: below –50°F

zone 2: –40° to –50°F

zone 3: –30° to –40°F

zone 4: –20° to –30°F

zone 5: –10° to –20°F

zone 6: 0° to –10°F

zone 7: 10° to 0°F

zone 8: 20° to 10°F

zone 9: 30° to 20°F

zone 10: 40° to 30°F

zone 11: 40°F and above

ZONE MAP

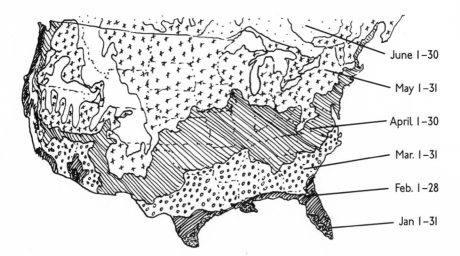

June 1-30

May 1-31

April 1-30

Mar. 1-31

Feb. 1-28

Jan 1-31

AVERAGE DATE OF LAST SPRING FROST

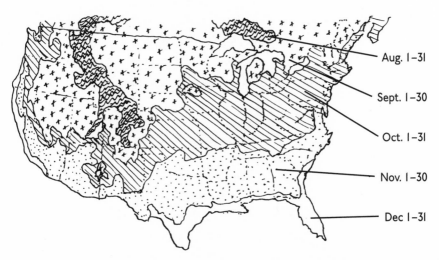

Aug. 1-31

Sept. 1-30

Oct. 1-31

Nov. 1-30

Dec 1-31

AVERAGE DATE OF FIRST WINTER FROST

When zeroing in on your hardiness zone, consider your particular conditions. Although I live in zone 4, plants on our farm in the upper Midwest are subject to harsher winter exposure than they would be if planted in town, where many trees and buildings provide additional protection. To compensate, farmers plant windbreaks, groves of shrubs and trees, which are often placed to the west and north of the farm-

19

stead because the worst winter weather often comes from these directions. Even so, I must plant fruits that are a half-zone or a whole zone hardier than I would if I were a "townie" in order to have them survive.

SUNLIGHT. When choosing varieties, allow for ample sun, depending on the needs of the fruit. Plants close to the north side of a building will be in almost total shade—which won't do for fruits; and plants on the south side of a building will get almost full sun, unless they are shaded by another building or tree. When full sunlight is recommended, it usually means at least six hours, although more is better. Shade part of the day is often tolerable for trees planted near the house on the east or the west. As long as the fruit gets good sun for a good share of the day, it'll do fine. Reduce the amount of sun, and you'll have less fruit, and the fruit might not be as flavorful or nutritious as it would be in full sun.

POLLINATION. Some fruits are self-fertile, which means that the plant can fertilize itself with its own pollen; others need a second or even a third compatible variety to ensure good cross-pollination. Be sure that the pollinators blossom at about the same time; it wouldn't do to have one in bloom and ready for pollen while the other is still in the budding stage with no pollen released. By the way, most berries are self-pollinating, which means that they don't need outside help, like bees, for fertilization. Be sure to get good information about the pollination requirements of the fruit varieties you're selecting.

AVAILABLE SPACE. Choose fruit that will fit the location even after it reaches full growth in maturity. Varieties vary greatly in size, so there's bound to be fruit that's suitable to your space limitations whether you're growing plants, shrubs, or trees. Pruning is another way to control size and shape, but for trees, it's best to start with a smaller or dwarf variety than to train a standard tree into a dwarf shape when its nature is to grow large. If you have only a long narrow yard, consider edging it with espaliered trees that grow flat like a fence without dominating yard space. Be aware that espalier does need to be pruned regularly, however, which takes a little time—but it's fun and easy to do.

DISEASE AND INSECT RESISTANCE. You can find out what problems are prevalent in your area by checking with your extension agent or at your local nursery. It only makes sense to purchase fruit varieties that are resistant to the diseases or insects common to your location.

YOUR TASTES AND NEEDS. Do you prefer sweeter apples over tart ones? Do you want strawberries that freeze especially well? Are you trying to use less added sugar, making the naturally sweeter hybrid rhubarbs your choice? Does your area tend to have early frosts, making a short-season hybrid more desirable? You can accommodate your personal tastes and needs when you raise your own fruits and berries.

NOTE: For years, my husband complained about planting trees. The reason? He said they were hard to mow around. The solution? Get him a zero-turning-radius riding lawn mower! It worked like a charm, and now even I enjoy mowing!

BARE ROOT STOCK OR CONTAINER GROWN?

I've bought lots of both kinds, and can say that both will work. Do be careful that trees or shrubs planted in containers have not become root-bound, that is, the roots have not grown round and round the container in a dense mass. Be sure that you loosen the roots at planting time, so that they grow naturally away from the tree, or they will continue growing in a circle and the tree will eventually topple due to lack of support.

If it's spring, it's time to plant trees—that's my motto, and I love to do it. It's my wish to have at least one specimen of every available variety! After all, one of the persuasive sales pitches The Farmer used on me was, "Just think, if you married me and moved to the farm, you could have all the gardens and orchards you want."

The year after we increased our grove to protect our orchard, a couple of the pine trees winter-killed. The Farmer suggested that I take his pickup to town to buy replacements, which I was only too happy to do. At the nursery, a shipment of wonderful stock was being delivered, and I was quickly able to choose the needed trees, which looked rather lonely in the back of the pickup. There was such a great selection of fruit tree varieties being unloaded right in front of me, that before I knew it, I had filled the entire pickup, inside and out! When The Farmer came in from the fields that night, he went to unload my purchases—and was astonished. He said I'd bought a forest! So now, when spring comes along, he won't let me have the pickup alone!

GROWING RANGE

Each fruit and berry entry specifies the recommended growing areas, and each of the varieties listed includes more detailed information about this. What's all the fuss about? Plants are particular about how much heat, and especially about how much cold, they will tolerate and live. The amount of cold is of the most concern for northerners, who must be careful not to plant something in an area that gets too cold, and for southerners, who must worry about plants getting enough cool weather in winter to go dormant.

For example, there are gooseberries hardy to –40 degrees F, red raspberries hardy to –35 degrees F, black raspberries hardy to –25 degrees F, and blackberries hardy to –15 degrees F. It's important to choose the appropriate varieties for your area.

If you are fond of particular fruits or berries but your winters are too cold for them, there are a few tricks that might enable you to help them survive temperatures five to ten degrees below their limit. Things like planting them where they'll be protected from the worst winter wind, insulating them with mulch, burying the canes in the ground over winter, and other tips that are mentioned in each fruit or berry entry. If all else fails, you can try growing the plant in a container and putting it in a protected building all winter.

Each fruit variety has differing needs for winter chill, which is required for the plant to be able to flower and fruit successfully. This is usually expressed as a minimum number of hours the plant needs to be under 45 degrees F. A plant that is said to have a high chill requirement needs more low winter temperatures; a low chill requirement means less. You can get more specific information for each variety from your nursery. Check with the nursery or your local Extension office for more information about growing specific fruits in your area.

When to Plant Fruit

Say "planting season" to a farmer and he'll instantly think "spring." Spring is the ideal time for northerners to plant everything—trees, shrubs, and plants—because everything they plant will have several months to get established before winter, which is our worst season.

In the South, the reverse is true. Summer is the worst season, because it is hot and dry, so fall is the best planting time, allowing the roots to get established over winter before having to go through a harsh summer.

About the Varieties

I've made no attempt to make my lists exhaustive, just to give some examples of plant material to consider. There are many, many more varieties available to you, and you can find information about them from your local Extension office; a local nursery; mail-order catalogues; or from the book, *Fruit, Berry and Nut Inventory* (see "Sources").

Why Grafted Stock?

I usually recommend buying trees from a reputable nursery, and you'll often find that they have been grafted. Why?

Because trees that produce wonderful fruit often have inferior root systems, and superior root systems are often found on trees that produce inferior fruit. So someone figured out that you could join the good tree top to the best roots and they will grow together and thrive so long as each trunk was the same diameter. This is called grafting, and you can easily spot the graft on the lower trunk of the tree because the area is thicker. There also might be a visible scar at the graft union.

Grafting increases the hardiness of trees, increases insect and disease resistance, and can be used to make a standard size treetop into a smaller dwarf or semidwarf tree.

Some trees have had more than one graft onto a trunk, in order to have a tree that produces more than one variety of fruit. This is tricky, because the fruit varieties must be compatible, and they must bloom at the same time and have the same hardiness. These appeal to people with yard space for one tree, yet who want, say, three or five different apple varieties. A multiply grafted tree is more successful in climates with less severe winters, because there is a risk that one or more of the grafts could winter-kill, leaving you with an oddly shaped tree.

Buying the Stock

Fruit trees, shrubs, and plants are available at your local nurseries as well as through mail-order catalogues. Signs of a healthy tree:

- If you nick the bark, you should see a bright green layer underneath.
- The branches should be springy, not brittle.

Standard trees are full-sized, often tall trees. Miniatures are very small trees, often made that way to grow as novelties in containers, without much regard for fruit production. Semidwarf and dwarf trees have standard treetops that have been grafted onto root stock that makes them grow smaller. Semidwarfs are usually 50 to 85 percent the size of standard trees, and dwarf trees are less than half the size of standards.

If you are considering fruit trees, I recommend the dwarfs. Why?

- You'll get a fruit crop much sooner, usually in two to four years, as opposed to the ten years it takes for standard trees to produce.
- The crop will be so much easier to harvest. You don't need tall ladders, and often you won't need any ladders at all.
- They bear full-sized fruit on small-sized trees.
- The tree is easier to spray, prune, and protect from birds.
- The trees take up less space but produce well for the space occupied.

AFTER YOU'VE RECEIVED YOUR STOCK

Do not allow the roots to go dry! But don't allow the roots to drown in too much water, either. It is a good idea to plant as soon as possible after receiving your stock.

It's not unusual for me to bring home one or two dozen potted trees or shrubs that need to be transplanted into the yard, and sometimes I can't plant them right away. If this happens to you, just stand them close together in a sheltered spot and water them daily. If the tree is in a burlap ball, cover the entire ball with mulch. If the wind is strong enough to knock the trees over, place bricks or cement blocks on the pots or against the root balls. You also need to consider pet protection. My cats sometimes like to sharpen their claws on the tender trunks, and once the neighbor's dog grasped a trunk in his teeth and ran down the lane, dragging the pot behind!

Preparing the Site

Just as a farmer always clears the field before planting, your first step is to eliminate whatever plant material is already in the area you've selected for your fruits and berries.

Existing bushes or trees will probably require heavy equipment. On the farm, these are removed with a tractor and loader bucket (driven by The Farmer). A heavy chain is wrapped around the tree or bush (done by The Farmer's Wife—note the uneven workload!), then attached to the bucket. When the bucket is raised, the tree or bush is pulled out, roots and all.

If you don't have a farmer or a friend with a tractor, you should probably get professional help with the heavy removal. Everything else you can handle yourself, by transplanting any plant material worth saving, or clearing it out in some way so that you won't have new growth coming from the old roots. Here are some possibilities:

SMOTHERING. Laying down opaque plastic, a tarp, or old carpet smothers grass and other plants and prevents them from getting sun-

light. Gardeners sometimes use old boards, even layers of old maga-
zines and newspapers. Just be sure to anchor whatever you're using
so that light can't penetrate and so the material won't blow away. It
takes a few days to a few weeks to be effective.

CHEMICAL SPRAYS. These kill everything. There is a two-week
delay before the plants are dead and you can use the soil. The chemicals need to be applied carefully, on a calm day, because they will kill
anything they come in contact with, including desirable plants. Be sure
to follow the directions exactly and protect yourself as instructed.

MANUAL LABOR. You can dig out the sod or other plants, but it
is a lot of work, especially if your soil is compacted and you're planting more than one tree or bush!

TILLING. This is my favorite
choice. If the sod is well established,
you might have to go over it several
times, then wait a week and repeat
the process. Rake out any root
clumps that aren't chopped up to
keep them from growing again.

COMBINATION APPROACH.
Some people like to combine methods, for instance using smothering
and tilling (the best combination!) or
using chemical sprays and then tilling the ground after two weeks.

Portable tiller

How to Plant Trees and Bushes

- Start when the soil is ready, otherwise delay planting a few
  days until it is workable. If the soil is soggy or cakes when
  you ball it in your hand, planting might compact it, making
  the soil too hard for the roots to penetrate and too dense for
  the roots to breathe in.

- Use a tiller to dig a hole twice as wide and a little deeper than the root ball. After you've loosened some of the soil, shovel it out and till it some more, altering the machine's direction. This is much easier than digging a hole in packed dirt by hand.
- Remove all tags and anything that would restrict the growth of the trunk or branches.
- If your tree or shrub arrives bare-rooted, soak the roots in a bucket of water for several hours before planting it.
- If your tree or shrub is growing in a container, remove it. An easy way to do this is to lay the plant on the ground, and press on the sides of the container as you rotate it, carefully avoiding harming the branches.

    NOTE: You may be instructed to plant the tree without removing the roots' covering, if they are balled in burlap, or they're planted in a papier-mâché container. After you've placed the burlap ball into the planting hole, unwrap the burlap and cut away the top third or else peel it back and bury it in the sides of the hole. For papier-mâché containers, cut off the rim, which can wick moisture away from the roots, and cut vertical slits on the sides and bottom of the container before planting.
- Loosen the roots so that they will grow outward, and not around the ball.
- Place the roots in the planting hole and spread them out so they grow naturally. Never bend the roots in a circle. Prune any damaged roots
- If planting a tree, position it at the same level as it grew in the nursery, with the graft above ground. Otherwise, the treetop will root and you'll lose the benefits of the grafted root stock, which include hardiness and the dwarfed size.
- Shovel dirt back into the hole around the roots, firming it so that there are no air pockets.
- When the hole is half full of dirt, pour in a couple of gallons of water.
- After the water has settled, check that the tree or bush is still standing straight.

- Finish filling in the hole with dirt. Mound and firm a ridge of soil around the hole to serve as a dike.
- Water the tree again.
- Mulch the base of the tree for at least the first two or three years. Then you can have sod, if it is kept mowed.
- Don't allow any livestock—hogs, cattle, horses—near the fruit or berry planting. They'll rub against it, eat it, trample it, or dig it out.

SHOULD I USE FERTILIZER AT PLANTING? Other than possibly mixing well-rotted manure in with the planting soil, I do not recommend using fertilizer at planting time. Why? Because we don't want to encourage the vegetative top growth at the expense of the roots, making the tree or shrub vulnerable to winter damage or even death. Also, if you overenrich the soil in the planting hole with chemical fertilizers, the roots might be discouraged from growing beyond the hole. Manure releases nutrients slowly, so it won't stimulate growth the way quick-acting chemical fertilizers do.

SPACING TREES

For the best cross-pollination, space compatible trees no more than three mature-tree-widths apart. Recommendations about spacing and pollination needs are given in each fruit listing, and you can check with your supplier about the specific needs of your tree.

If your soil is not deep and rich, you can space the trees a little closer because they won't grow quite as large. But don't space them so close that they shade each other or limit air circulation. Air circulation dries off the foliage, which prevents disease, so if you live in a humid or cloudy area, you might want to space the trees a bit wider to encourage circulation.

STAKING TREES

Some gardeners like to stake their trees, to keep them upright and straight. I usually don't do it. For one thing, I'm always planting lots of trees. I feel it's better for the tree if it's not staked. It will adjust and toughen up to the existing conditions, and some experts feel that the motion in the treetop stimulates growth in the roots. If you get a lot of wind that threatens to overturn the taller trees, you'll need to stake them until they are established. Otherwise, consider leaving them alone unless they don't grow straight on their own.

Container Growing

With a little extra work, you can grow fruits in containers. It is one way that you can have fruit from trees or shrubs if you lack a yard or if your climate is wrong for that type of fruit or berry.

Apricots are a popular choice because they will produce fruit in containers better than all the other trees. Any fruit in this book can be container-grown if you choose a dwarf or miniature variety. Other possibilities include:

PONDEROSA LEMON, a small tree with grapefruit-sized fruit. Or try the Meyer lemon, which has normal-sized fruit. They can flower any time and the harvest can be year-round.

MANDARIN ORANGES, on trees six feet tall. Consider the Owari Satsuma variety.

KUMQUAT, a very attractive tree only four feet tall, with delicious small fruits that are eaten rind and all—I slice them and add them to vegetable stir-fries. Try the F. Hindsii or the Nagami varieties.

MEXICAN LIME, a bushy eight-foot tree with willowy branches that produce small, round, seedless fruit.

BONANZA PEACH, for delicious full-sized fruit on a four- to five-foot bushy tree.

FIGS, which can be started from seeds taken from store-bought dried figs, but require patience as they take three months to germinate.

Most of these are self-fertile, and some produce seedless fruit if pollination doesn't occur. Citrus other than lemons need a higher temperature than is available in homes, for the fruit to develop its sugar content. The exceptions are the miniature citrus, which grow only two feet tall, that are specially developed for containers. These will occasionally fruit, but you'll have to hand-pollinate them.

Dwarf Cavendish bananas are successful in containers. The plant gets five to eight feet tall, and the edible fruit is six to eight inches long. It must be grown in a large container, no less than two feet in diameter; get maximum amounts of sun; and always be in temperatures over 65 degrees F. After the fruiting is over, the trunk will die and should be cut off. New shoots will start from the roots; remove all but one to start the plant over.

Container-grown citrus takes from seven to fourteen months from pollination to maturity, and this long period of time makes them more vulnerable to fruit drop.

All container-grown trees have a tendency to drop their flowers and their fruit prematurely. Even so, they can be worth growing for the beautiful foliage alone—which is why I have an eight-foot lemon tree in my living room.

HOW TO PLANT CONTAINERS

For the container, you can use almost anything—pots, barrels, plastic waste baskets, livestock watering tanks, even old bathtubs—so long as there is proper drainage and so long as there is sufficient room for the roots. The larger the container, the better for the roots, but also, the heavier and harder it is to move. Be careful about wood; untreated wood probably won't stand up well, and chemically treated wood can leach harmful elements into the soil, and thus into the fruit. Whatever you decide to use, here are the steps to take:

- Don't transfer a tree from a small pot into a much larger container. It's better to plant it in a container two or three inches larger than the existing roots, and gradually move up to a container appropriately sized for the mature plant. Start bare-root trees in a five-gallon container, no smaller.

- Put drainage holes in the bottom of the container. (Use a saucer to protect your floors from the drained water if the container is indoors.)
- If possible, raise the container off the floor or ground by placing it on bricks or cement slabs.
- Line the bottom of the container with landscaping fabric, to filter the draining water, keeping in the soil.
- Place a one- or two-inch layer of crushed rock on top of the landscaping fabric. I sometimes use nonbiodegradable Styrofoam packing peanuts, to lessen the container weight.
- I recommend using purchased potting soil that has been sterilized to prevent insect and disease problems. You can mix in compost and/or sand, if needed.
- Place a layer of potting soil in the bottom of the pot and then set the root ball on top of this layer. Check to see if the tree or shrub is positioned properly, relative to up and down and also to its depth in the soil. You want the soil line to be perhaps two inches below the top of the container, and you want the plant at the same level it was previously growing.
- In subsequent years, if you've reached the maximum-sized pot for your tree, pull the tree roots out of the container and check them. If they look root-bound, trim off about one inch from the sides and bottom of the root ball with a knife, and repot it in the same container using fresh soil.
- If you are pruning the roots, you must also prune back the tops a little, to keep the two in balance. Pruning the tops does not automatically require a root pruning, however.
- Mulch the exposed soil, to make it look more attractive and to hold in moisture, especially if the container will be outside. Or, cover the surface with two inches of small stones—this is especially desirable if the pot is large and you have cats who like to dig. Include a few large rocks to add weight to the base, if the tree will be in wind.
- If desired, you can grow flowers, vegetables, or plant combinations like strawberries and white alyssum around the base of the tree or shrub. This is quite attractive, especially if you include some trailing varieties. In addition, the foliage will

protect the fruit roots from baking in the sun, and will reduce moisture loss from the sun. Select plants that are not heavy feeders and that do not have large root systems that would interfere with those of the tree or shrub.

- If you intend to have the tree outdoors part of the year, consider burying the pot partly or fully in the ground. This will better anchor the tree or shrub against strong winds and help retain moisture.

WATERING CONTAINER PLANTS

VERY IMPORTANT: If you have container trees outdoors in the sun, you must water them every day, or perhaps twice daily, to keep the soil from drying out. Do this even if you get rain, because the canopy of the tree or shrub might prevent the rain from falling into the pot. You can test the moisture level by sticking a finger into the soil.

Indoor container plants also need a steady supply of moisture, although you might get by hand-watering them only once or, at most, twice weekly.

Never allow the plant to wilt, but don't let it sit in water-logged soil, either. If you've provided well for drainage, you can water generously with no problem. In time, you'll know how much and how often to water each plant.

If possible, do not use treated water.

FEED CONTAINER PLANTS ONCE OR TWICE A MONTH AT QUARTER STRENGTH.

Seaweed or fish emulsion fertilizer is a good choice for container plants, but it does have a faint odor. If this bothers you, switch to a natural product from the Gardens Alive! catalogue or use a commercial solution.

PRUNING CONTAINER PLANTS

Planting in containers will automatically dwarf a tree, due to the roots' being restricted. You will still need to do some pruning, perhaps even severe pruning, to control the size of your shrub or tree and to keep it in bounds for its location, whether outdoors or in a room inside. Pruning is best done from December through February. I've often added the pruned branches to flower arrangements, especially when entertaining dinner guests.

Be aware that severe pruning can limit fruit production, because the fruit often appears only on year-old wood. A better choice would be to minimize the need to prune by selecting stock that's already dwarfed or miniaturized.

Lemon trees need lots of pruning, as I can attest, to keep a tidy shape. The branches tend to cross and grow irregularly in strange directions, and you'll also want to cut off the 1¼-inch-long thorns that grow along the trunk.

MOVING CONTAINER PLANTS

If you live in cold climates, you will not want to leave your containers outside through the winter, because freezing and thawing cause expansion pressure that can destroy them, to say nothing of the plants they contain.

Tropicals do not need winter chill and cannot tolerate any frost; they must be relocated to a warm area prior to the temperature drop. Other fruiting trees and bushes will need some winter chill; that is, they need to be in a sheltered spot for a period of time, usually in temperatures below 45 degrees F. This can be accomplished in an unheated garage or other building, or perhaps on an unheated porch. If the area doesn't get severely cold, that is, it remains below 45 degrees F but above freezing, the tree or shrub will stay dormant all winter. Otherwise, you should bring the tree or shrub indoors sometime after the chill requirement has been met, especially if your winters are very cold.

When relocating any shrub or tree to room temperature indoors, place it in the area where it will get the most possible sun, avoiding heat registers.

When it is time to move the shrub or tree back outdoors, place it in a shaded area so that it can adjust, gradually moving it into full sun over a one- or two-week period.

An easy way to transfer heavy pots is to slide them on a trolley or two-wheeled handcart. Attach the pot to the cart with bungee cords, and it will be secure to wheel inside or outside.

Ongoing Care

PROTECTING YOUR ROOTS

If you notice that any roots become exposed above the soil, be sure to cover them up with additional soil.

Don't till close to trees, even if you have your tiller set to shallow depth. Tilling can damage the roots or even kill the trees. You might try the Cape Cod hand weeder tool, which glides just under the soil surface, easily removing weeds.

You can put flowers under the trees, but choose types with shallow roots and be careful not to disturb the tree roots by digging. It's best to plant seeds or seedlings that require a very small hole.

Cape Cod Hand Weeder

I've planted daylilies under many of my trees. They are very hardy and make a tidy ring around the trunk.Once they're established there is no weeding necessary, they stay neat without landscape edging, and mowing next to the plants won't harm them.

PROTECTING YOUR
TREE TRUNKS AND SHRUBS

The first year or so, you might want to put tree protectors on the trunks. These will guard the more delicate bark from damage, prevent sun scald, and discourage deer, which are attracted to the immature bark. Do not use the kind that spirals around the trees; despite claims to the contrary, this type of tree protection can end up strangling the tree, which I had happen to a weeping mulberry, to my great regret. The best protection is the type with a vertical slit so that the tree can force it open as it expands in width.

Do not use a rotary whip or motorized grass cutter near shrubs or the trunks of trees. A friend used a whip to trim the grass under his new trees, accidentally cutting the trunks right at ground level, girdling—and killing—them all.

When mowing, be very careful that the mower doesn't cause damage to the trunks. Applying a layer of mulch helps create a buffer around the base of the tree. It's recommended that you allow a three- to six-inch space between the mulch and the tree trunk. Or you can buy wonderful flat, donut-shaped tree bases made of ground-up recycled tires. They come in several sizes and are heavy enough that the mower suction won't lift them. They allow air and moisture to pass through freely, yet are a weed barrier (available from Gardener's Supply, see "Sources").

SPRAYING FRUIT TREES

For information about the pests in your area, and suggested spraying schedules, you can check with your local Extension or nursery. I recommend using the safe horticultural oils that will prevent insect damage to the fruit. These sprays are quite effective, especially when applied at the right time. I would rather suffer a little insect damage than risk eating fruit that's been sprayed with poison.

The first dormant or horticultural oil spraying should be done in early spring before the trees bud out and when the wind is low and the temperature will be above 45 degrees F for at least eight hours after spraying. Getting all these conditions at the same time is very difficult here in Iowa, and I have to be ready to scramble as soon as the weather cooperates. Depending on the spray you select, you will probably do subsequent spraying as the summer progresses. To do this, you will need some equipment.

Unless you have a large orchard, you will need a hand sprayer with a one- or two-gallon capacity, the type that uses a hand pump to compress air in the tank to force the spray out of a hand nozzle. When buying the sprayer, get extra hose length so that you can reach the tops of dwarf trees with the spray wand. Also, buy face masks and eye goggles, and be sure to wear gloves, long pants, and a long-sleeved shirt for personal protection, even when using the safe organic sprays.

To make spraying faster and easier, The Farmer used to put me in the back of his pickup and drive me up and down the rows of trees. But that ended when The Farmer got a new pickup, because he does-n't like to clean the spray residue off his paint job. So now he puts me and my sprayer in a beat-up old wagon that he says I can't hurt, and pulls me with his oldest, smallest tractor! Either method works great, because I am elevated and moving around the branches without having to carry the heavy tank. And it's easy to periodically rock the spray tank, to keep the solution well-mixed.

An alternative to using a pickup or a tractor is to use bungee cords to attach the sprayer body to a two-wheeled handcart, which can be purchased inexpensively. You can wheel this around the orchard and park it as needed, freeing you to concentrate on operating the spray wand. It works well for all but the tallest trees.

After you've finished the spraying, open the air release valve on the sprayer before removing the lid to rinse out the whole unit with water. To clean out the hose, run water through the spray nozzle for quite a while, particularly if you lengthened the hose.

Insects and Disease

Insects not only can harm the fruit and berries before we have a chance to harvest them, but they can also open them up to decay and airborne organisms that can cause disease. The insects themselves can also transmit disease on their bodies. But before you declare war, please understand that there are many insects that benefit your fruits and berries, so you want to use an approach that won't eliminate them along with the troublesome insects.

Besides chemical sprays, there are many other kinds of products you can use. For example, horticultural oil sprays stop overwintering pests before they come out of hibernation. Insecticidal soaps handle aphids and other bugs. Bt or MVPII sprays take care of worms and caterpillars, and the birds can still eat them without harm (see Gardens Alive! in "Sources").

Besides purchased products, you can try making your own insecticidal soap by adding three tablespoons of a mild dishwashing soap (not the kind with degreaser) to a gallon of water. Stir it up and spray the plants thoroughly; wait one or two hours, then rinse it off. You will probably need several applications for bad infestations.

For diseases, here are some homemade sprays you can try:

- Baking soda spray is a general fungicide that works on anthracnose, blights, and mildew. In one quart of warm water, combine one teaspoon of baking soda and one teaspoon vegetable oil or mild liquid dishwashing soap (not the kind with degreaser). Shake often while spraying, and be sure to get the tops and bottoms of leaves.
- A 50-50 solution of skim milk and water combats mildews.
- Hydrogen peroxide, the 3-percent solution commonly available in stores, can be sprayed on plants for bacterial and fungal problems. Be careful not to breathe the spray. If the problem is confined to a few large leaves, you can dip several cotton balls in the peroxide and wipe them with it.

Remember, birds and bats eat lots of insects. Enlist nature's help by putting up a bat house, purple martin house, or some other kind of bird house. If you can tolerate it, encourage nonpoisonous garden snakes or even toads. Don't be quick to get rid of wasps, because they kill lots of harmful insects or their larvae, as do bees and bumblebees, which also pollinate our crops.

You can get information about the insects and diseases that are troublesome to fruits and berries in your area and the products to use on them from your Extension or your local nursery. Or you can order many effective, safe products (including a bumblebee house) from the Gardens Alive! catalogue (see "Sources").

Pest Management

RODENTS

Chemical traps are often used. Some gardeners sprinkle ammonia at the base of the plants or use hot pepper spray around the plant, which act as repellents. Sometimes bone meal is recommended, but I've found that it actually attracts some undesirable creatures.

Moles are really beneficial animals, because they eat grubs, not plant roots. Try using bacillus to eliminate the grubs, and the moles will go elsewhere. Or try this formula from Doc and Katy Abraham in the newsletter for the Hobby Greenhouse Association: one part castor oil and an equal part of liquid detergent, plus a little warm water. Beat this into a foam. To use it, stir two or three tablespoons into a watering can of warm water and pour it over the soil where the moles are troublesome. Repeat the dousing until the moles leave.

The best solution for other rodents? Consider cats—I never have a problem!

BIRDS

Scare tactics include using scarecrows or images of birds' natural predators like hawks, owls, or snakes. The birds get wise to these after a while, and so they need to be rearranged frequently. One garden friend swears that to be effective, you must do this on a moonless night, in the dark, when the birds can't see you.

Barrier methods include covering the developing fruits or berries with netting, which works well but can be a nuisance. My suggestion: Tie the plastic bags you get at the grocery store onto the trees and shrubs. They will move in the slightest breeze and make a soft crackling sound that the birds dislike. For short plants like strawberries, you can tie the plastic bags onto stakes inserted in the ground.

The other option is to raise enough fruit so that there is an abundant crop for both humans and birds—and remember all the good that birds do for us as they consume a diet of insects.

DEER AND OTHER WILDLIFE

Deer, in particular, can be very destructive to all types of fruits and berries. I lost a tree last winter, not due to the severe weather, but because a hungry deer girdled it; that is, chewed off the bark all the way around the trunk. It was an unusual tree variety that I wanted to save, and I noticed that the girdling was above the graft, so I cut off the top of the tree just below the girdling in very early spring. This stimulated bud development. What I'll do is allow three of these to grow into new branches, eventually pruning out all but the best one to stake and train to become the new tree. I've done this several times over the years, with great success—the trees have become straight and tall and you can't tell the tree was ever girdled. However, my tree expert warns me that these trees are weakened and might one day topple in a strong wind.

So, it's far better to prevent the damage in the first place. How can this be done?

Some gardeners put up a fence as a barrier, but to be effective the fence must be at least eight feet tall. And it must go into the ground several inches to prevent rabbits from getting under it. But if snow piles up around the fence, both deer and rabbits will have no trouble going over it in the winter.

Repellent methods include mothballs, baby powder, strong-smelling bar soap, special spray mixtures that usually include pepper or raw eggs, and human hair or dog hair suspended in nylon hose or spread on the ground. Some gardeners say that a line of human urine just outside the area you want to protect is effective—but somehow I can't get The Farmer to take care of this for me!

Aside from the urine and the eight-foot fence, which is just not practical or cost-effective to build around twelve acres in snow country, I've tried all these suggestions and many, many more. I can say that none of these works for long and all require some effort. They must be renewed periodically, including after every rain, which is quite a nuisance if you have many fruiting plants to protect. Every year our deer population increases and the deer seem to get bolder and bolder about eating everything. So what are we to do?

My all-time favorite recommendation: Use grocery bags, as suggested for birds. It works wonderfully well! I tie the bags to the trees and shrubs so that they hang low enough to hit the deer's head. If there is a breeze, the motion and the sound act as a repellent. Even if there isn't a breeze, the deer and other wildlife are nervous about being near the bags. Now, the only trees in my orchard that sustain rabbit or deer damage are the ones that have had their bags torn off by the wind. To prevent this, I tie several bags in each tree, using bags that are all the same color, so it looks a bit neater and deliberate.

Tying the plastic bags to stakes just above the ground even keeps the wildlife, including rabbits, from eating my strawberries. The bags cost nothing, are easily replaced, and are environmentally friendly. Try it, it works!

Weeding

SMALL WEEDS. If you have a small weed growing among the shoots of your fruit plant or bush, pull it out by hand or use a hooked hand-weeding tool that gives you a lot of control in a very small space. Or use a traditional hoe or, better yet, one of the newer, smaller types that are easier to operate. Use sliding motions, skimming just under the surface, and the weeds will disappear. Be careful not to go too deep, or you risk damaging the roots of your fruit crops.

SMALL OR MEDIUM-SIZED WEEDS. For these, the tiller works well, especially between rows. Set the tines for shallow digging. If you purchase a portable tiller, you can work in small spaces yet still maintain control so that you don't chew up desirable plants.

LARGE WEEDS. If the weed becomes too large, it probably has a well-developed root system. Pulling it by hand—even if you have the strength to do it—could damage fragile fruit roots. Instead, cut off the weed at ground level or even below, using nippers, loppers, or a corn knife. The weed might grow back again from the roots; just keep cutting it off and eventually it will die. Of course, it would be far easier to have gotten rid of this weed before it had a chance to become so established—but I know how quickly weeds can grow, seemingly overnight!

The weeds you remove can be used as mulch, tilled under as "green manure," or added to the compost pile, unless:

- The weed has seedpods. Even if they are immature, the seeds might be able to germinate. Burn or otherwise dispose of these weed plants, seeds and all.

- The weed has underground runners. I'm thinking of a vigorous quack grass that's just awful if it gets a foothold in your garden. You can pull the weed, even dig out the roots, but if only a one-inch length of the white runner remains, it can sprout and grow in the garden or in the compost pile.

ABOUT CHEMICAL WEED CONTROL. Be aware that:

- Some leave toxic residues on the fruit you'll be eating.
- Some are harmful to the environment, including your well water, animals, and beneficial insects. An expert once persuaded me that a granular herbicide would take care of my weeds without harming children, pets, or the environment, so I tried it. Two cats burned their paws by walking on it, and when they licked it off, the ingested chemicals killed them. Don't let this happen to you!
- Some are so potent that if even one tiny drop gets on a single leaf, the whole plant, tree, or bush will die.

WHEN TO USE CHEMICAL CONTROL

- For weeds like quack grass. It's impossible to sift through the soil to remove every single bit of the underground runners that sprout from even the shortest segment, so the only way to eradicate this pest is to use chemicals. In fact, I used chemicals on quack grass just before I wrote this section. We covered all the nearby plants with sheets of plastic before spraying. We waited until the spray was completely dry, and we were very careful not to let the plastic touch any plant as we removed it.
- For weeds with extremely deep, persistent root systems that can stubbornly send up new shoots even if the plant is repeatedly cut down or dug out. If allowed to grow unhampered, Canadian thistles get as tall as a person and send down roots that go very deep, perhaps eleven to thirteen feet. Once they get a foothold, the only way to eliminate them is with a systemic chemical that the plant transports down to the root system. (It's too bad, because they have lovely purple flowers

and are the favorite food of our state bird, the yellow finch, which is one way the weeds are spread! Once in a while, I'll run across a blooming thistle and put the flowers in a vase in the house—it never fails to get a rise from The Farmer!)

Farmers are required to keep noxious weeds under control, and have penalties for failing to do so, because the seed generated by just one plant can start an infestation of thousands. Our counties have rigs to spray all the roadside ditches to kill any weeds, and a weed commissioner goes around checking to see that we are in compliance. It's sad because we've lost our native plant diversity, including many wildflowers and other useful plants. One example of a plant rarely seen now is the milkweed, the bane of my childhood. We'd have to walk through our fields to pull weeds by hand, including many milkweeds. Ironically, I now allow milkweeds to grow in my gardens (don't tell the weed commissioner!) because monarch butterflies need them to lay their eggs and provide food for their caterpillars.

PREVENTING WEED SEEDS FROM GERMINATING in the first place saves a lot of trouble. Mulch is one method, but there is an additional approach. I recommend an all-natural product developed here in Iowa from corn gluten. It's a yellow-orange powder that, when spread on the ground, prevents germination without harming fruit plants, children, pets, or the environment. It works well, providing you apply it in spring and fall before the weed seeds have sprouted. Understand that it prevents the germination of all seeds, not just weeds, so wait until your desirable seeds have all sprouted into plant seedlings, which aren't bothered. This product is available from Gardens Alive! (see "Sources").

Pruning

WHY PRUNE? It's done to:

- Remove dead or damaged wood. NOTE: If a major limb breaks and splits the trunk as it falls, but it is still attached, you can sometimes repair it. When this happened to one of my trees, I encased wire in segments of old garden hose and wrapped it securely in several places around the truck and also the branch. I left it in place for one year, watching the tree to make certain the wire wasn't strangling it. When I removed the supports, the tree had grown together again, and today you can't tell there ever was a break.

- Prevent crossed branches from rubbing against each other.
- Thin out dense growth that keeps the sun and air from penetrating the tree's interior.
- Eliminate branches that are too horizontal or that are growing downward; these will not be able to support the weight of fruit.

Nippers, loppers, handsaw, and bow saw

- Remove the water sprouts, or the fast-growing, vigorous branches that shoot straight upward in awkward places.
- Remove suckers, or shoots that come up below the graft, which are from the root stock and not true to the top. If allowed to grow, they will eventually kill the grafted top.
- Shorten branches and encourage new growth in an outward direction.
- Space the lowest branches at the desired height above the ground.
- Shape the tree.

Don't overprune, however, because you might be cutting out the most productive fruiting parts.

Also, the leaves are needed to manufacture carbohydrates for the plant's energy. Losing too many leaves in one season will reduce the next year's crop, and might even jeopardize winter survival.

When you prune, leave the collar, or the ripple of bark at the base

43

PRUNING TO A BUD

I. Cut is too close to a bud; the bud might die.

PRUNING AN ENTIRE BRANCH

I. Do not leave a stub.

2. Cut is too far from the bud; stub will die and risk health of the tree.

2. Cut just above the collar.

3. Just right; the cut is about 1/4 inch from the bud.

3. The scar will close with new growth from the outside to the center of the wound.

of each branch, on the tree. It has chemicals in it that help the wound to heal and that prevent the opening from being susceptible to disease or rotting.

NOTE: Use clean nippers that have been wiped with a bleach-water solution, to avoid transmitting disease.

WHEN TO PRUNE

Pruning should be done in late winter, preferably before the tree or bush has budded, so the plant won't have wasted energy in growing leaves that are cut off. Pruning while the tree or bush is still dormant allows you to better study the branch structure, to see what needs to be done. Never prune in the fall because the plant won't have the chance to heal before winter.

You should prune anytime you see dead or damaged limbs or suckers or water sprouts, the vigorous upright shoots growing from the roots or around the graft, or on the lower trunks of trees.

PRUNING AT PLANTING TIME

FOR TREES: You want to make sure that the tops and roots are in balance. If the roots were cut at the nursery, but the top was not, you might want to do a bit of pruning, because the roots may not be large enough to provide water and nutrients to the top. This could cause some branches, or even the entire tree, to die.

The reverse, too many roots for the top, is actually desirable for planting outdoors. Root pruning is done only to remove damaged roots or to straighten out tangled roots that will not grow naturally outward. The exception to this is discussed under "Container Fruits."

FOR SHRUBS: Generally, they need less pruning than trees. Specific instructions for each fruit or berry is included under each listing.

Espalier

When a tree is trained to grow flat against a wall or fence, it is said to be espaliered. Strict pruning and training produces an attractive shape that takes up very little space. Sometimes a whole row of espaliered trees is used to form a living fence. Since the tree has limited top growth, thus reducing the crop, it concentrates its energies on producing large-sized fruit. It takes several years and some effort to train a tree into espalier, and the care must be ongoing to maintain the strict espalier shape for the life of the tree.

An east or west wall is the best location for an espaliered tree. A north wall doesn't give the tree any sun. A south wall might spur the tree to bud out too early in the spring, or even during winter warm spells. Before deciding on an espaliered tree, consider what upkeep the wall requires. For example, is it painted? This will be difficult to do after you have a tree growing against it.

I recommend using dwarf apple trees, because the fruits form on spurs instead of on one-year-old shoots that must be properly maintained for fruiting.

Before you begin:

- To aid you as you select and prepare the proper site for espalier, be sure to read the preceding sections about locating fruit trees on your property, preparing and enriching the soil, and how to manage too much or too little soil moisture.
- Be aware that you may have to replace the soil for several feet down if you are training an espalier against a building; during construction, the worst dirt is often placed against the foundation.
- Get reliable advice concerning the pollination needs of the tree varieties you're considering.
- Purchase very hardy stock from a reliable nursery. To minimize the chances of winter-kill, get a tree that can survive conditions more harsh than it will ever receive in your area. It would be disheartening and difficult to remove a tree you've spent years training against a wall, or to replace one in a whole row of perfectly espaliered trees.

HOW TO ESPALIER

- Buy a young, dwarf, nursery-grown tree that has an upright growth habit and not much top development. The trunk should look very healthy and unblemished.
- Before you plant the tree, have a plan for the support system you'll be using. After the tree is established, you'll no longer need the support, which can be removed or, in the case of wood, allowed to rot away. We used synthetic eight-foot poles tied together at the top and anchored in an upside-down V in the ground. Crosspieces are later tied to this frame. (For an alternate support system, see NOTE below.)

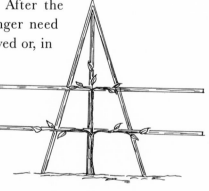

A-frame for espalier

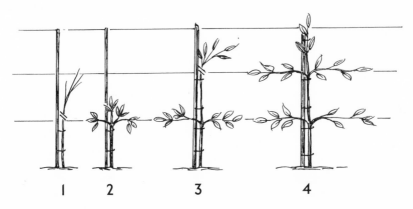

1. Cut back the top.
2. New shoots grow.
3. Cut back the top.
4. Train new shoots.

TRAINING ESPALIERED TREES

- Till the planting area thoroughly and deeply, scooping out the loose soil as you let the tiller dig the hole. Mix in well-rotted manure or compost, and sand, if needed.
- Place the tree in the hole, carefully positioning it so that the trunk will be at least six to nine inches away from the wall or fence. Plant it at the same depth it was growing at the nursery.
- Loosen the root ball and, if growing the tree against a fence, fan the roots out so that they will radiate naturally in all directions, or so that they all fan away from a wall or building.
- Position the support securely in the planting hole, avoiding the roots. You might want to anchor the top of the support to the wall or fence for more stability.
- Fill in the planting hole, carefully tamping to remove any air pockets.
- About eighteen inches above the ground, cut off the top of the tree, just above an area where there are three shoots clustered together or there are three buds that will grow into new shoots. (I know, it is hard to make yourself decapitate a perfectly healthy tree!)

- Directly behind the now-shortened tree trunk, position a third eight-foot-long pole vertically, attaching it to the top of the V support frame. Secure the tree trunk to this third pole by wrapping a strip of pantyhose in a figure-eight around the pole and tying it around the tree trunk. This will cushion the bark from rubbing against the support. Do not tie down the top three or four inches of the trunk or you might impede the growth of the new shoots.
- Water the tree well, and keep it watered, as needed.
- Allow the new shoots to grow until they are eight to twleve inches long.
- Attach a horizontal crosspiece to the support frame, behind the new top shoots. You can use anything that will give you a straight horizontal line, like bamboo, synthetic garden poles, etc., or string wire horizontally against the wall, securing it to the V support, and attach the shoots to the wire (see NOTE, below).
- Carefully, gently, bend down the two outside shoots until they are at a right angle to the trunk, so that one is going to the left and one is going to the right. Secure these to the crosspiece with strips cut from nylon pantyhose.
- The third shoot will become the new trunk. Train it to grow straight up by tying it with a figure-eight to the pole supporting the trunk.
- Allow the new trunk to grow about two or two and a half feet above the first horizontal crosspiece. In early spring, when the tree is just beginning to bud, measure up fifteen to eighteen inches from the first crosspiece and cut the trunk just above three buds.
- Allow these three new buds to grow shoots eight to twelve inches long, then train them to a second crosspiece positioned fifteen or eighteen inches above the first one.
- Repeat this process until the tree is at the desired height.
- As needed to provide wider support for the horizontal branches, extend the crosspieces by attaching more bamboo. Support the extensions by tying them to sturdy stakes

put in the ground near the wall or fence, or keep tying branches to the horizontal wires.

- As needed, prune out any other shoots except those you're training into horizontal branches. Be careful not to remove the fruiting spurs, however, and do not remove any leaves growing from the branches, only shoots.

NOTE: Although I prefer the upside-down V-shaped support described above, you can also place sturdy eight-foot posts in the ground on either side of the tree as far as you want the horizontal branches to reach, and string 10-gauge wire between the stakes. Or, use large eye-screws on long shanks attached to the wall or building to support the horizontal wires. The developing tree is then attached to the wires. Never attach the branches directly to the wall so that they touch the wall surface; leave a space between the wall and the tree so that air can circulate, fruit can develop normally on the back side of the branch, and training and pruning are easier to accomplish.

Other flat espalier patterns include the palmette verrier, where the horizontal branch tips are trained to grow vertically; the fan, which is especially suited to trees that fruit on one-year-old shoots, like the peach; and the Belgian fence, or a row of trees that each have only two branches that crisscross each other.

Espalier can be used in other interesting ways. For instance, two rows of trees can be trained to arch until the branches meet at the top and sides, or a circle of trees can be joined to create a living gazebo. Both of these need to have well-shaped supports, usually of welded metal rods. I have plans to develop several new espalier designs here on the farm. (But don't tell The Farmer. It's better if he knows about only one project at a time!)

Certain trees, including the apple, have the interesting ability to grow together as if they were one tree with multiple trunks. You can scrape off the bark where the branches from two trees touch, secure them, and they will permanently join together, just as if they were grafted. This technique is used to strengthen the Belgian fence, the arched row, and the gazebo.

ESPALIER PATTERNS

Gridiron

Palmette Verrier

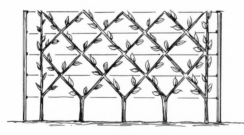

Above:
Single T, Double T, Horizontal T

Palmette Oblique

Belgian Fence

U

Double U   Triple U

Pollination

Some fruits or berries are divided into male and female plants, and you need one of each to produce fruit. Others require a second variety nearby in order to cross-fertilize the blossoms and produce fruit. Still others are able to be self-fruitful. Sometimes fertilization occurs from gravity or the wind, but often fruits and berries need the help of bees or bumblebees.

A parasite has destroyed much of our bee population. All too often, humans panic when they see bees and rush for chemicals to kill them. The result has been a serious shortage of bees, which not only affects our honey supply, but also jeopardizes our fruits and berries and other crops dependent on bees for spreading pollen.

There is some good news, however. The bumblebee, which is different from the honey bee, is making a comeback. Bumblebees, scientists say, are too large and heavy to be able to fly with their small wings. Yet fly they do, in stronger winds and cooler temperatures than honey bees.

Bumblebees go peacefully about their business in the garden, rarely attacking humans unless deliberately provoked. They usually nest underground in abandoned mouse or snake holes, or you can provide them a place to live in very early spring. Bumblebee houses are available for purchase at garden centers, or you can order them from the garden supply catalogues I've listed in the "Sources" section.

Fruiting

Most of the fruits and berries I've listed come into production early, sometimes even the first season. However, it is recommended that you remove the fruit from fruiting trees the first year, and thin it the second year, so that the energy goes into getting the roots established and the branches have a chance to grow strong before they have to support the weight.

Thinning Fruit

Sometimes fruit trees get into a pattern of bearing well every other year. You'll hear farmers say it's an "apple year" or it's "not an apple year." Many things contribute to creating this pattern, but the main theory is that many flowers got destroyed somehow: perhaps strong winds blew them off, or a severe winter or a late frost killed that year's blossoms. Since the flower embryos for the next year are developed in the current season, the theory goes, the tree then puts all its unused fruiting energy into developing the next year's blossom embryos, thus creating a surplus. These result in a large crop the following year.

Experts say you can help even out the crops by reducing the quantity of immature fruit during the bumper year. This is done after the natural June drop, when part of the fruit is sometimes spontaneously aborted from the tree. Where appropriate, I've given you the recommendations for thinning in each fruit listing.

Having said all this, I must now confess that I never thin my fruit. It would be quite a job, considering the size of our orchard. We have enough trees that we always have fruit, although some years I may not have any of a particular variety, and other years it might come in great abundance.

How to Harvest

Fruiting plants like strawberries, cantaloupe, watermelon, and even rhubarb are easy to harvest. Fruiting shrubs are not difficult to harvest, either, especially if you've followed the directions for pruning and training them. Fruiting trees are also easy to harvest, if you've followed my advice and planted the dwarf varieties. Most of the fruit can be handpicked from the ground. For the higher fruit, you can:

- Stand on a ladder, which you rotate around the tree.
- Stand on the ground, but use a picking tool attached to a long pole. This is okay for one or two

trees, but a bit of trouble for an entire orchard.

• Stand in the back of a pickup truck and easily reach even the highest fruit, effortlessly putting it into five-gallon buckets in the truck bed.

Guess which method we use? The Farmer drives the pickup truck between the rows of fruit trees, and I can harvest the top fruit on half the tree before he repositions the truck.

NOTE: Be very careful about moving a pickup truck with a person in the back. To be safe, the person should be sitting on the floor of the pickup, with his or her back against the cab. Never sit on the side of a moving pickup, and do not sit on the wheel well inside the bed of a moving pickup. People have been badly injured, even killed, by not following these safety precautions.

The fruit listings that follow will give you specific information on when and how to harvest each fruit or berry, and what to do with the crop after harvest. Be sure you don't leave ripe fruit or berries on the tree, bush, plant, or on the ground below. It will attract insects.

Winter Protection

If you live in an area that freezes, remove the ridge around your newly planted trees and shrubs that serves as a well to contain water. Water accumulating there can freeze, damaging the trees or shrubs.

What else should you do in preparation for winter? Anything that protects the plant tops or the roots from succumbing to severe weather is called winter protection.

BARRIERS are usually in place before planting. You evaluated the predominant direction of the wind and then took advantage of the placement of walls, fences, buildings, trees, hills, or anything that will prevent the harsh wind from directly hitting the plant. Anything that is marginally hardy for your area should receive some sort of barrier protection. If you wish to grow a fruit or berry that is not hardy in your area, consider planting it in a container that can be moved into a building, for complete barrier protection.

ALUMINUM FOIL is effective in preventing mice and rabbits from eating the bark of young trees. Wrap it around the base for at least three feet—more if you get higher snow, because rabbits can hop on top of a snowbank to eat above the barrier.

INSULATION protection includes snow cover and mulch. Both of these can prevent the top of the plant, as well as the ground and roots below, from being subject to high or low temperature extremes, performing much as house insulation does in summer and winter. Snow is not always available when it's needed, during the harshest cold weather, so some type of organic material might be necessary in the coldest climates, like mulch over the roots and base of the plant, and leaves or straw loosely piled over it. Beware of packing the material too densely or the plants will smother; even dormant plants need to be able to breathe.

It's interesting every year to study how our snow melts. Our mulched areas always emerge first, even if the snow cover is higher there. This is because the mulch keeps the ground below from getting as cold as ground that wasn't mulched.

If you are worried about getting a late frost in early spring that might kill off fruiting blossoms, especially on peaches, nectarines, and apricots, place a thick layer of mulch over the roots in late winter. This will keep the ground from warming, perhaps delaying the blossom time long enough to avoid frost damage.

OTHER WINTER PROTECTION MEASURES include such things as wrapping tree trunks and laying cornstalks or dead canna plant material over vining plants. These coverings aren't exactly insulation, but act more like a windbreak and shade protection, and keep the plants from coming out of dormancy during a warm sunny spell in the middle of winter, only to be harmed by the return of cold weather.

MOISTURE in the ground. Don't forget: Dry soil is the leading reason a plant, tree, or bush, especially when young, dies over winter. A good deep drink before the ground freezes will help guarantee winter survival.

Once established, your fruiting plants, trees, and shrubs will be better able to withstand weather conditions without protection. It's neither practical nor desirable to cover entire trees or bushes with mulch over winter. But you can take steps to aid the fruit or berry in its winter survival. More detailed winterizing tips are given in the individual listings.

My Garden Book

Get a large three-ring binder and keep track of every single plant, bush, and tree that you plant, so that you don't find yourself wondering what kind of apple tree you've got or which blueberry variety you need in order to pollinate the one you have.

Record the date and year, the variety, the qualities of the variety; and why you chose it. What care should it get? When is the fruit or berry ripe and ready to harvest? Is the fruit good fresh? Frozen? Cooked? Is winter protection necessary? What ongoing care does it require?

Be diligent about recording this information all in one place—you'll be glad you did!

KITCHEN NOTES

Tips for Storing Fruit and Berries

Keep hand-harvested fruits separate from windfall fruits. Fruit that has fallen on the ground will be more mature and will make the harvested fruit ripen faster. Use the windfall fruit first.

Never store fruits and vegetables together. For example, don't combine apples and potatoes in a fruit cellar—the ethylene gas from the apples will make the potatoes sprout. Some gardeners who lack cool cellars store their fruit in Styrofoam chests in their unheated garage through winter.

When buying a new refrigerator, consider keeping your old model, or purchase an inexpensive used one to store fruit. Turn the temperature dial a little colder than is normal and most fruit will keep a long time.

TO WASH FRESH FRUITS, use cool water. Warm water might soften the fruit and even cause it to bleed. In general, rinsing is better than soaking the fruit, because the fruit is less likely to become waterlogged. Look in the specific fruits and berries listings for additional suggestions.

TO REMOVE FRUIT STAINS, particularly when they're caused by the darker berries like blueberries and mulberries, just rub the stain with the inner rind of a lemon. This works especially well on counters and sinks, and also on hands and under nails.

Serving Ideas for Fresh Fruits

WHIPPED CREAM is a great topper for any fruit. For every cup of heavy whipping cream, add 2 to 4 tablespoons of powdered sugar, ½ to 1 teaspoon of vanilla extract (optional), and 1 tablespoon of dry powdered milk. (The powdered milk keeps the whipping cream firm for two or three days in the refrigerator.) Beat the ingredients together to the consistency of a fairly stiff whipped cream. If the cream, beater, and mixing bowl are well chilled, the cream will double in volume when whipped.

NOTE: A cordless blender is a quick and easy way to make whipped cream—and the cleanup is effortless!

FRUITED WHIPPED CREAM is easy to make by adding about ½ cup of fruit puree or fruit butter to the plain whipped cream, above, and whipping it until stiff and blended.

CINNAMON WHIPPED CREAM is delicious on any fruit, especially peaches and the sweeter apple varieties. To make it, follow the instructions for plain whipped cream, above, adding ½ teaspoon cinnamon per 1 cup of heavy cream.

FRUIT DIP can be easily made with softened cream cheese or sour cream. Just stir in brown sugar to taste and serve it with fruit pieces. If using the dip with apples, pears, or peaches, you can add a little cinnamon and vanilla. The dip keeps a long time stored in the refrigerator.

MARSHMALLOW FRUIT DIP can be easily made with 8 ounces of softened cream cheese blended with one small jar of marshmallow cream.

FRUIT DRESSING can be made by blending together 6 ounces of cream cheese, a 5.5 ounce can of apple juice, and ¼ teaspoon cinnamon. Serve over fruit pieces.

FRUIT PARFAITS are very pretty desserts—and so easy!

- Layer whipped cream and your choice of fruit in parfait glasses.
- Or substitute yogurt for the whipped cream; if using plain yogurt, you can stir in about 1 tablespoon of honey per cup.
- Or substitute vanilla pudding for the whipped cream layer.
- Place attractive, bite-sized pieces of reserved fruit on top of the whipped cream as a decoration, perhaps flanked by fresh mint leaves.
- Other topping ideas: toasted nuts or shredded coconut.

FRUIT GLAZES: Simmer canned pineapple or apple juice with a dash of cinnamon or two or three whole cloves and 1 or 2 tablespoons of butter per cup of liquid for 5 or 10 minutes. Remove the whole cloves, cool, and serve the glaze over fresh fruit. Besides adding flavor, this glaze prevents the fruit from turning dark.

FRUIT BUTTER TOPPINGS: Place fresh fruit in individual serving dishes. Dribble 1 or 2 tablespoons of a fruit butter (recipes for fruit butters are included in the listings) over each serving and top with a dollop of whipped cream. Sprinkle your favorite nuts over the whipped cream. Fast and terrific!

Notes about the Fruit Recipes

All the recipes included are fast, easy, and absolutely delicious! They're inspired by the way farmwives used to cook for their hard-working men who consumed huge meals to fuel their intensive back-breaking labor in the days before farm machinery.

If your crew no longer labors in the fields all day, you might prefer to reserve sugared desserts for special occasions. Fresh fruit is the regular dessert of choice at our house unless we're having guests—and somehow The Farmer finds people to invite frequently!

ABOUT THE INGREDIENTS

ZEST. This is the very outer skin of lemons, limes, and oranges, which can be added to other fruits as an accent flavor. First wash and dry the fruit, then either grate it or use a tool called a zester, being careful not to get any of the whitish pith underneath the outer skin, as this is bitter. Measure zest by lightly placing it in a measuring spoon. Zest can be frozen in airtight containers for later use.

SUGAR. I use sugar with a light hand. This allows the fruit flavor to predominate, and it's healthier to cut back or eliminate the refined flour and sugar in our diets. Also, some hybrid fruits are naturally sweeter than others, requiring less added sugar in a recipe. So I often express the amount of sugar as a range, as in "⅔ to 1 cup sugar." I suggest starting with the lowest amount the first time you try a recipe, unless you have a big sweet tooth, in which case you might even want to exceed my highest range.

SALT. You'll notice that my recipes seldom list salt as an ingredient, but they will benefit from a dash or pinch of salt, which enhances the flavor.

ABOUT THE ICE CREAMS

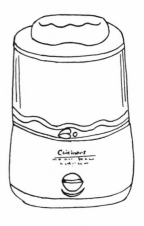

Instead of using the old-fashioned ice-cream makers that take lots of time, ice, and salt, consider buying one of the newer models that freeze a quart of ice cream in 20 minutes or less, without ice or salt. There are several reasonably priced models on the market now; some of them require occasional hand cranking, some are electric. All are easy to operate and to clean.

I prefer the type of ice-cream maker with a separate liner that you freeze, so that you don't have to use salt and ice. Just pour in the recipe, and in about 20 minutes, you're ready to serve wonderful ice creams or ices. Although I was satisfied with my hand-cranked model for many years, I recently switched to an electric one, and I must say it's better, especially for the fruit ices, which come out smooth and fluffy like ice cream.

My recipes can be made without an ice cream machine, but it will take more time and effort, and the texture will be softer. Here's how: Put the mixture in a covered metal bowl in your freezer. Remove it after 15 minutes and beat well. Return it to the freezer. Repeat this several times until the ice cream or ice is firm enough to serve.

Fruit and berry ice creams are so easy to make from the simple— and delicious—recipes I've developed. You can start from scratch and be eating a fabulous dessert in less than 20 minutes!

If you are raising your own fruit and haven't used dangerous chemicals, you can leave the skins on—which are a source of nutrition. Removing the skins does sometimes make a smoother ice cream texture; for example, in the Easy Pear Ice Cream. A way around this is to make the ice cream from the cooked fruit sauce, leaving on the skins; they will puree smoothly.

You'll notice that I don't use eggs in my ice cream recipes. The traditional farmwife of old would use raw eggs. When potential health risks were discovered, we began cooking the egg mixture. This meant extra steps, more dishes to clean, and a delay while the mixture cooled. So after experimenting, I've come up with simple yet terrific-tasting ice cream recipes that are true to the traditional taste, and that are safe because they are egg-free! And the only pan to clean is the food processor bowl. You'll be eating fresh ice cream in less than 20 minutes!

The very best flavor comes from real cream, which farmwives favored because it was always available from the milk cows, and also because it's delicious! Some experts are saying that natural fats are healthful (except in combination with quantities of refined flour or sugar), but if you prefer, you can use the substitutes I've listed, like plain yogurt, which you can purchase in reduced-fat form. But consider trying the original recipes first, reducing portion size, if necessary. These recipes are very quick and very, very good. Not to be missed!

If you have leftover ice cream, place it in a freezer container. Place plastic wrap directly on the surface of the ice cream; then seal the container with the lid to keep ice crystals from forming. Your ice cream will be frozen hard. Before you eat it, allow the container to sit on the counter so that the ice cream will soften; then stir it before serving.

NOTE: If desired, you can substitute frozen fruit or use fruit sauce instead of pureeing the fresh fruit for the ice creams and the ices. Adjust the added sugar downward a bit to compensate for the sugar in the fruit sauce.

ABOUT THE ICES

If you are short on dairy products, or if you prefer not to use them, try the ices, which are rather like a sherbet or sorbet in texture and flavor. At fancy restaurants, ices are served between courses to "clear the palate." My fruit and berry ices are even quicker to make than the ice creams, and they taste great!

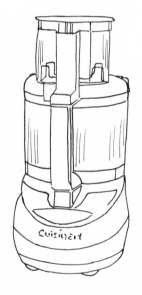

As with all of my recipes, I prefer to use the least amount of sugar possible. But I express the sugar measurement as a range, so that you can adjust it higher if you like a sweeter flavor, or perhaps need extra sugar to compensate for fruit that's tarter than usual.

As with the ice creams, if you have leftover ice, place it in a freezer container and lay plastic wrap directly on the surface before adding the lid—this will prevent large ice crystals from forming. Take the ice out of the freezer prior to serving so that it will soften. Then beat it by hand or return it to your ice cream maker and crank it a few times to restore the texture.

ABOUT THE SAUCES AND POACHED FRUIT

Farmwives made large bowls of fruit sauces or poached fruit and served them with the main course more like salad than dessert. They could accompany breakfast, dinner, or supper—the meal vocabulary of farmers—or be served along with the midmorning or midafternoon lunch. Farmers had hearty appetites to fuel their long hours of hard labor!

The sauces or poached fruits can also be used like a relish on meats, or as a topping for cakes, biscuits, or ice cream. They are quick and easy to make, and they freeze well—which is a great way to use an overabundance of ripe fruit.

ABOUT THE BUTTERS

As an extremely busy farmwife, I cannot devote time and attention to making jams and jellies because of all the steps they take: cooking the fruit to just the right stage with the right amount of pectin, sterilizing jars and canning them in a hot-water bath, being certain that the jars seal properly, to name a few. Although few people want the fuss, mess, and time commitment for all this, most of us would still like to have homemade preserves, because they taste so-o-o good!

Years ago I discovered the answer—make fruit butters and store them in the freezer! It's so simple! You just cook the fruit with a little sugar and perhaps some added flavoring until it is somewhat thickened, place it in freezer containers, and you're done! The butters contain far less sugar than jams or jellies, thus emphasizing the great fruit flavor. Using your own fruit at the peak of freshness ensures that your homemade butters are more flavorful than any jams or jellies from the store.

The butters can be used in many ways: on bread, muffins, biscuits, rolls, waffles, pancakes, crepes, yellow or white cakes; as toppings for ice cream; and layered in parfaits, and they can even serve as glazes on meats and poultry! Or bake muffins with a surprise center by putting half the batter in the pan, making a well in the batter, dropping in a spoon of fruit butter, covering each muffin with the remaining batter and then baking as usual.

If you are making fruit butters in quantity, you'll want to invest in a quality kettle to cook them in. I recommend stainless steel that is fairly heavy; thin pots scorch easily. Or use a large spatter-ware roasting pan, the type you use for your Thanksgiving turkey, putting it on your largest burner or even spanning two burners. Never use aluminum because the acid in the fruit will react with the metal, causing an unpleasant change in the color and flavor of the fruit. Although it's handy to purchase a pan with a nice-fitting lid for other purposes, you won't need the lid when making the butters because they thicken by evaporation.

Some people like to use a slow cooker without a lid, although I've never tried it. If you do this, I recommend covering the pot with a screen spatter guard to not only prevent spattering, but also to keep insects out.

The butters are simmered slowly on low heat. For a firmer butter, lengthen the cooking time. But don't judge the butter while it's hot, because it will thicken as it cools. It also tastes sweeter after cooling.

For freezing information, see below.

ABOUT THE PIES

My mother, her mother, and her Swedish grandmother all insisted that the secret to a great fruit pie was to generously dot the filling with pats of butter. Real butter, not margarine. And it's true! I use perhaps 3 or 4 tablespoons on an average pie.

When baking pies, I recommend that you place a catch tray or piece of aluminum foil with raised edges on the lower oven rack and bake the pies on the middle rack of your oven. If your pie should overflow, it won't be a bother; fruit filling can be difficult to clean.

The filling recipes I've included can be placed in your favorite homemade crust (my preference) or a purchased crust. I tend to make large pies with generous fillings, so if there is more filling than your pie tin can accommodate, just place the extra on another crust, fold it over, seal it, and bake it, and you've got a tart.

Other Fast and Easy Ways
to Use the Pie Filling Recipes

Fruit Cobbler

1. Place the filling in a greased pie pan or 8 × 8-inch or 9 × 9-inch square baking pan or divide the filling into six or eight custard dishes or ovenproof ramekins.
2. Cover the filling with pastry crust or a biscuit topping (use purchased biscuit dough or the following recipe). Bake as usual.

Biscuit Topping

1. Combine in a mixer bowl:
   > I cup flour
   > I tablespoon sugar
   > I teaspoon baking powder
   > ¼ teaspoon baking soda
   > ¼ teaspoon cinnamon
   > Pinch salt
2. Cut in 4 tablespoons softened butter. Don't overmix; it will look loose and coarse like meal.
3. Make a well in the flour mixture and add 9 tablespoons of buttermilk (½ cup plus 1 tablespoon). Stir until barely combined.
4. Flour the counter and turn out dough. Pat it slight smaller than the shape of your cobbler container. Do not overhandle the dough. Cut the dough into squares and lay the squares over the filling so they are not touching. (If using custard dishes or ramekins, place one dough square in each.)
5. Bake at 375 degrees F about 20 minutes or until the biscuits are lightly browned and the filling is bubbly. Serve warm with cream or whipped cream, if desired.

Fruit Crisp

1. Place the pie filling in a greased 8 × 8-inch or 9 × 9-inch square baking pan or divide the filling into six or eight custard dishes or ovenproof ramekins.
2. Sprinkle a crumb topping over the filling. Recipes follow:

Crumb Topping

1. Combine with whisk until crumbly:
   1 cup sugar
   3/4 cup flour
   1/2 cup softened butter
2. Spoon over pie filling and bake at 350 degrees F for 40 minutes or until the fruit is done.

Oatmeal Topping

1. Combine:
   3/4 cup oatmeal
   3/4 cup flour
   1/4 cup brown sugar, packed
   1/2 cup butter, softened
2. Place over pie filling in a 9-inch baking dish (or use a pie plate, but there might be extra topping) and bake at 325 degrees F for 40 minutes or until the fruit is done.

General Notes and Procedures for Putting Up Fruits

Canning is the traditional farm method for preserving foods. My mother (and her mother and grandmother before her) used to can hundreds of quart jars of produce yearly, and I remember how pretty they looked in our basement storage room, especially my favorites, the blue jars. The wonderful taste of home-canned goods is unbeatable. Traditionally, the farmwife would do the canning in her summer kitchen—a separate one-room building on the farmstead—to keep the heat from canning away from the main house. With the advent of fans and central air-conditioning, farms no longer have a summer kitchen, yet in my canning days, the house would heat up faster than our air-conditioning could keep up. The Farmer bought me a supplemental window unit for the kitchen, which helped but was a hassle to put in every summer and take out every fall. Canning is hot, time-consuming, and hard work, no matter what! Sadly, I no longer have the time to do it.

But I can recommend a great alternative to canning—freezing. It's fast, easy, and doesn't heat up the house. It also preserves more nutrients in the food and nearly matches canning for flavor and texture, if done correctly. Frozen fruits can be used like fresh fruits in most recipes. If you freeze the fruit with sugar, you might want to decrease the amount of added sugar in the recipe.

Consider purchasing a stand-alone freezer if you find yourself with an abundance of produce you'd like to put up. I have two—one is an upright freezer the size of a large refrigerator, and one is a chest freezer. Remember: A full freezer uses the least energy.

POINTERS FOR FREEZING FRUIT

Be sure to freeze mature fruit, not fruit that's underripe, which might get bitter and discolor, or fruit that's overripe, which might turn to mush when it's thawed. Look under each fruit listing for specific freezing techniques.

Small fruits or **fruit pieces** usually freeze quickly, within two to four hours, if placed in a single layer on jelly-roll sheets or trays. The pieces should not be touching. After they're frozen hard, you can transfer the loose fruit to freezer containers in premeasured amounts to make your favorite recipes. Or you can place the frozen fruit in freezer bags. If the plastic seems thin, it's wise to double-bag the fruit to prevent freezer burn. Always squeeze out all the air you possibly can.

Fruit sauces can be frozen in containers. Be sure to include the liquid with the fruit. Allow ½- to 1-inch headspace for expansion.

Fruit butters freeze extremely well in containers. Allow headspace for expansion.

If desired, you can freeze **fruit puree**, either cooked or uncooked, for future use.

However you choose to freeze your produce, be sure it's well-packaged and frozen quickly or the quality of the fruit will suffer. Pack the packages in the freezer in single layers until they are frozen solid, do not stack the unfrozen packages in blocks, which take longer to freeze and affect quality. Once the food is frozen, you can organize the packages in blocks for efficiency and to save space. You'll probably want to store all packages of one fruit together.

The food in the freezer should be kept at 0 degrees for best results. If freezing very many packages of fruit, you might want to set it at –10 degrees to hasten the freezing, and return it to 0 degrees once everything is frozen solid.

Labeling Is Important

Freezer bag manufacturers often put built-in labels on freezer bags suitable for writing directly on the plastic. For containers, use stick-on computer or mail labels or wide tape and write on them with a fine-tipped permanent Magic Marker. Include the type of fruit and what it is (i.e., "cherry butter" or "apple pie filling"), and the date it was frozen. Store the oldest packages at the top or front of the freezer, so that they will be used first.

Freezer Packaging

PLASTIC BAGS: When freezing loose fruits, I recommend the heavy plastic bags especially made for freezing that are self-sealing (as opposed to using a wire twist tie), because they lie flat, conserving freezer space; the food freezes quickly, because it's spread out flat; it's easy to eliminate air as you seal the package; the bags are disposable, eliminating cleanup for reuse; and the bags are inexpensive. I recommend placing the filled bags on cookie sheets or in cake pans until they are frozen, so that you don't end up with awkward shapes that are hard to store.

RECYCLED PACKAGING: Another option is the plastic cartons you get when you buy yogurt, cottage cheese, sour cream, etc. Clean them thoroughly before use for freezing. These cartons are an especially good choice for anything with liquid, like fruit butters. Leave ½- to 1-inch headspace for expansion when the liquid freezes. Best of all, these cartons are free, and you are recycling instead of throwing away a resource. The only downside: the cartons are usually round, and don't conserve freezer space as well as if they were square.

FREEZER CONTAINERS: You can buy square-shaped plastic freezer containers to maximize freezer space. These recyclable cartons must be hand-washed and stored for reuse. The biggest downside? When putting up dozens or hundreds of packages, as I do, purchased freezer containers become costly.

VACUUM SEALING: Air in the package causes oxidation, which causes food to deteriorate in the freezer. One way to eliminate more air than you can possibly squeeze out of the package by hand is to purchase a vacuum-seal machine and special plastic sleeving material. You fill the plastic with the desired quantity of prepared produce, and the machine sucks out the remaining air and heat-seals the end of the plastic, usually in one operation. I've done this and it worked well, although the machine didn't stand up to much use. Perhaps the machines have been improved since I last tried them.

FREEZING FRUIT PIES

This is still a common activity for farmwives, especially when there is an abundance of fruit that needs to be put up in some way. I have done dozens at a time, when fruit is in season.

There are several ways to put up fruit pies:

- Assemble the pies complete with their top and bottom crusts and then wrap and freeze them without any prebaking. This method ties up your pie plates until the pies are eaten, unless you buy disposable foil tins. I do not recommend storing the pie without a tin because it usually results in damaged crusts.

- Make the pies and partially bake them until they are about three-fourths done, then cool, wrap, and freeze. Later, remove the pies from the freezer and finish the baking. This method also ties up the pie tins until you've eaten the pies; disposable foil pans are a possible solution.
- Freeze only the pie fillings. This is my favorite method when I'm doing many pies in production; it saves a lot of time both at the freezing stage and later at the assembly stage because the filling is already prepared! Directions follow.

How to freeze pie fillings:

1. Make the pie filling, adding a little more thickener (the flour, corn starch, or tapioca) than is usually called for in the recipe. Why? Because freezing breaks down the fruit's cell walls, releasing more moisture than usual from the fruit.
2. Line the pie plates by crisscrossing two 20-inch lengths of plastic wrap.
3. Add the pie filling. Then cover it by raising the outer lengths of the plastic and wrapping them over the pie.
4. Put the pie plate with the filling in it into a large zippered freezer bag and freeze it until it's solid.
5. Remove the frozen pie from the zipper bag. Gently pull the pie plates away from the filling, and return the wrapped filling to the zipper bag and freeze. This is a quick method to freeze a lot of pies!

How to make a pie from a frozen filling:

1. Remove the filling from the freezer.
2. Line the same-sized pie pan with pie crust.
3. Peel the plastic from the still-frozen filling.
4. Sandwich the filling in the crust and bake it in the oven till done. Don't wait until the filling has thawed. Easy and fast!

NOTE: Do not freeze custard-type pies, cream pies, or pies with meringue. (The exception is pumpkin pie, which can be frozen after it's baked.)

FREEZING FRUIT BUTTER

Freezing fruit butter is so easy! Save plastic cottage cheese cartons, yogurt cartons, or sour cream cartons and lids. Allow the fruit butter to cool to room temperature and fill the clean cartons to within ½ to 1 inch of the top. (This allows headspace for expansion of the fruit when it freezes.) Cover tightly with the lid, label and date each container, and place them in the freezer. My fruit butter recipes are ever so much faster and easier than the traditional methods of making fruit preserves.

To use frozen fruit butter:

- Take it out of the freezer the day before and thaw in the refrigerator, or
- thaw small containers on the counter as you prepare a meal, or
- place the sealed container in a bowl of hot water that is changed every few minutes, or
- loosen the lid and place the butter in the microwave for 20-second intervals, stirring often.

To remove the frozen butter from the carton:

- Check that the lid is sealed, place the carton upside down in the sink, and pour hot water over it. After a few seconds, gently push down on the bottom and it will release.

FREEZER MANAGEMENT

Keep a paper record of what you put in your freezer, either by taping a poster board on the freezer door or by hanging a clipboard on the wall nearby. Be specific and tally not only the number of items put in the freezer, but record each item as it is removed.

Make it a point to use all the fruit packages in the freezer within one year or less, usually by the next spring, before you start harvesting the next year's crop. Eating fruits and berries that have been properly frozen after eight or twelve months is not harmful, but the quality might suffer.

Spring is also a good time to empty out the freezer, defrost it if necessary, and scrub it thoroughly in preparation for the new harvest, like those early strawberries. You can transfer whatever frozen foods you have remaining to another freezer, or place them close together in laundry baskets and wrap the baskets well with blankets, throw rugs, or towels. The food will stay frozen for the time it takes to do the spring cleaning.

To hasten the defrosting of the ice buildup in the freezer, you can blow hot air on it with a hair dryer, but be careful to avoid electric shock.

A good freezer-cleaning solution is three tablespoons of baking soda per quart of warm water. Use this to scrub all the freezer's walls and shelves, then wipe them dry

If any odors linger after you've cleaned out the freezer, just place an opened box of baking soda inside and they'll be absorbed.

APPLES IN THE GARDEN

Say the word "apple" and most people instantly envision a bright red fruit with sweet, whitish flesh so juicy and crisp it crackles when you bite into it. It has bumps on the top and tapers to smaller bumps at the bottom. It is aromatic and the skin might have faint stripes or yellow freckles. You'd be thinking of the most common apple in the United States—the Red Delicious.

We almost didn't have the Red Delicious. It was an unwanted "volunteer" seedling growing in an Iowa orchard in 1872, and the owner cut it down twice but it kept growing. When the owner sampled one of its fruits, he thought it was the most delicious apple he'd ever eaten—hence the name.

There are over a thousand different apple varieties, with a wide range of colors, flavors, and attributes. With such a selection, apples can be grown nearly everywhere.

Description

Apples are a long-lived tree that come in dwarf, semidwarf, and standard sizes. I recommend the dwarfs because they produce full-sized fruit that's easily harvested, and they'll start fruiting in only one or two years.

Some apple varieties are better eaten fresh and not cooked; others are better cooked and not eaten raw; and some are great for all purposes. The Red Delicious is usually eaten raw because the pulp is sweet and it's too soft and loses its shape when cooked. Jonathan, Rome Beauty, and Golden Delicious are often chosen for cooking because they have firmer, tarter flesh, although The Farmer prefers to eat tart apples.

LOCATION: If there isn't room for an orchard, apple trees are usually planted as a focal point in the yard. You can fit three or four dwarfs in the same space a standard tree would take. Dwarfs are easier to fit into the landscape, either singly or as a row, perhaps along the property line. If you have a long driveway, consider planting a row on one or both sides.

One tree trunk can have up to five different apple varieties grafted onto it—which is great for people who want variety but have a small yard. I don't recommend planting this type of tree in the far north, however, because they are more susceptible to winter-kill.

If you don't have room for even the smallest dwarf tree, you can plant a pole apple, which is only eight feet tall and two feet wide. Or consider espalier, which takes even less space because the tree can be planted flat against a building or trained into a living wall on the edge of your property. Lacking a yard? Dwarf or pole apples can be grown in containers on your deck or balcony.

NOTE: Apples will set a good crop without a pollinator, so you can get by with one tree, if that's all you have room for, but cross-pollination increases the crop and will happen if your neighbor has an apple or even a crabapple tree.

GROWING RANGE: Any area where winter gets below 48 degrees F, because apples need some winter chill.

CHILL REQUIREMENT: Most apple varieties need between six hundred and a thousand hours of temperatures between 32 and 45 degrees F, but low-chill varieties have been developed.

SOIL: Most soils are suitable for apples, so long as they won't be in standing water.

MOISTURE: Apple roots go down deeply to get the moisture, which makes watering less critical for apples than for other fruits. Water generously the first season, if you don't get at least one inch of rain per week. After that, the trees probably won't need to be watered, unless they are container grown.

LIGHT: Full sun.

PLANTING SEASON: Spring.

HOW TO PLANT:
- Since grafted trees are the most successful, purchase nursery-grown stock.
- Follow steps in "Garden Notes" section for planting fruit trees.

PLANTING DISTANCE:
- Ten to twelve feet for dwarf trees
- Twenty feet for semidwarfs
- Forty feet for standard trees

SUPPORT: None is needed unless the tree needs staking to withstand strong winds.

ONGOING CARE: In the early spring and throughout the summer, spray the trees with horticultural oil to combat insect problems.

PRUNING: Prune to remove tangled branches, damaged wood, dangling limbs, watersprouts, and suckers at the base of the trunk. Leave the short twiggy spurs; these are for fruit production.

WINTER PROTECTION: Take steps to prevent animals from damaging the trees.

VARIETIES INCLUDE:

- **Anoka**, which produces large yellow-skinned fruit with red stripes that has crisp white flesh. Early season harvest. Zones 3–8.

- **Cortland** apples have a vivid red skin and snow-white flesh that doesn't turn brown. The apples are wider than they are tall and mine always grow to be quite large. Great eaten fresh or in salads, and great for cooking. Especially good for making sauce. The dwarf version of this tree is attractive, stays short and wide, and has strong, spreading branches that tend to droop. Harvest is midseason. Zones 4–8.

- **Fuji**, which keeps well even when stored at room temperature. The skin is yellow-green with an orange-red blush, and the fruit ripens late. Zones 5–9.

- **Golden Delicious**, which has a similar shape and size to the Red Delicious, with a different skin color. It has a long bloom season and can pollinate other apples with different bloom times. It has a creamy-colored flesh that doesn't turn brown. Good eaten raw, in salads, and it cooks well. The tree is attractive, with upright branches and a rounded form. Bears young. Harvest is mid- to late season. Zones 5–9.

- **Haralson** produces large red apples with a golden blush and crisp white flesh. Good for eating and cooking. Stores well. Midseason harvest. Zones 3–8.

- **Jonathans** are small to medium apples with a rich flavor that are used for cooking and are eaten raw. The trees bear heavily; the fruit is mature in mid-season. Zones 5–8.

- **McIntosh** produces medium to large fruit that has white flesh and bright red skin with carmine stripes. Crisp and very juicy, it's good fresh or cooked. Harvest is early to midseason. Zones 4–8.

- **Prairie Spy** is a late bloomer, so it is the choice for areas with late frosts. The apples are yellow with a red blush and they store well. Late harvest. Zones 3–8.

- **Red Delicious**, the most common of all apples. The fruit is medium to large in size, with deep red skin and crisp, sweet, and juicy flesh. Great eaten raw and in salads; not the best choice for cooking. Harvest is mid- to late season. Zones 5–8.

- **Red June** is a gourmet juicing apple that makes great cider and is also good for pies and eating fresh. The white-fleshed, red-skinned fruits are small, but the crop is large. Zones 4–10.
- **Rome Beauty** is usually raised for pies and sauce and is an excellent baking apple because it holds its shape. Although not usually eaten raw, I find it good when it's fully ripened. Trees produce heavy crops at an early age and the fruit keeps well in storage. Harvest is late. Zones 5–8.
- **Wealthy**, an old-timer, has medium to large apples that can be used raw or in cooking. It has a long bloom period in mid-spring and is a good pollinator. It has a fine texture and is tender, tart, and juicy. Makes excellent sauce. Harvest is early to midseason. Zones 4–7.
- **Winesap** is another smaller apple that is great for eating raw, in salads, or for cooking. It also stores well into winter. Midseason harvest. Zones 5–8.

FRUITING: First harvest is usually one to three years after planting dwarfs, standards can take five to ten years, and semidwarfs produce a first crop somewhere in between.

Experts recommend hand-thinning the fruit to one apple every six inches, and that the apples shouldn't touch each other. I must confess that I never bother with this and it works out fine. It would be quite a job with the number of trees I have in my orchard!

YIELD: It varies greatly, depending on the variety, tree size, and growing conditions, but dwarf trees produce one or two bushels, semidwarfs produce four or five bushels, and standards produce five to ten bushels per year.

HARVESTING: Apples are ready for harvest from late summer into late fall, depending on the variety. The best way to tell if they're ready is to bite into one! While you're at it, look at the seeds; dark-colored seeds are a sign of maturity.

To pick an apple, twist it off, but leave the twiggy branch it's growing on—that way you'll have fruit the next year.

Try to harvest the fruit with the stems still attached—these will keep longer. A missing stem means there is an opening for the fruit to rot. Separate out the fruit picked without stems and use them first.

Bruised apples don't keep as well; try not to bruise them during harvest or else use the bruised fruit first. (You can cut off the bruises.)

Apples in the Kitchen

Apples continue to ripen after being picked, so store them in a cool place to slow them down and then they'll keep longer.

I store apples in five-gallon buckets in our unheated garage into early winter, covering them with an old quilt when the temperatures get into the teens. (Boy, does this make our garage smell good!) Some people have success using old ice chests or Styrofoam storage containers on cool porches. For fresh apples through winter, I store them in our second refrigerator—this year we ate the last of the crop in April. A friend individually wraps each apple in a small piece of newspaper before storing them, and says this keeps them crisp.

What I don't keep in the garage or the refrigerator, I freeze into sauce, pies, or butters. With ten apple trees in our orchard, I could write a whole book just on storing and cooking apples!

Freezing Apples

DRY PACK METHOD

1. Wash and quarter the apples, cutting them in slices if desired; peeling is optional, but recommended if you'll be using the apples later for pies.
2. Dip the fruit in a solution of ¼ cup lemon juice per gallon of water (or, if freezing only a small amount, the ratio is 1 tablespoon of lemon juice per quart of water).

3. Drain the apples and freeze in a single layer if you want the fruit loose, or pack pre-measured quantities directly into freezer bags or containers. Seal, label, and freeze.

OTHER: Apple butter, applesauce, apple pie, and apple dumplings all freeze well if properly packaged. The apple dumplings can be frozen unbaked, without the syrup, in large freezer bags. Remove the quantity desired, make the syrup, and bake while the dumplings are still frozen, allowing a little more baking time.

Eating Apples

Everyone knows how great apples are eaten out of hand. They can be added to salads, used with dips, and, depending on the variety, they can be cooked into many wonderful dishes.

NOTE: The flesh of most raw apples, when exposed to air, will turn brown. To avoid this, sprinkle with orange, lemon, pineapple, or lime juice or ascorbic acid, or dip into water with lemon juice in it.

Salad Combinations

- Sliced apples and grapefruit or orange sections.
- Diced apples with shredded carrots and raisins.
- Apple slices, chopped cranberries, diced celery, and orange sections.
- Diced apples, diced tangerines, and crushed unsweetened pineapple.

Apple Appetizers

Cut apples into wedges. Spread the cut side with all-natural peanut butter. Roll in chopped nuts.

Easy Apple Salad

Wash apples and core and cut into chunks. You can add finely chopped celery, chopped pecans or walnuts, sliced or slivered almonds, shredded coconut, small marshmallows, or even other kinds of fruit, like grapes, pears, etc. Stir in enough whipped cream, mayo, or yogurt to coat all the fruit. Chill and serve within a few hours. (Otherwise the fruit liquids might cause the whipped cream to become runny.)

Panfried Apples

Core and slice unpeeled apples. Toss into a skillet with hot melted butter. Stir-fry until apples are tender-crisp. Drizzle with a little honey and serve.

Easy Apple Cabbage Stir-Fry

Cut cabbage into wedges, then cut the wedges into chunks. Core and slice an unpeeled apple, preferably one with red skin. Melt a little butter in a skillet and add the cabbage and apples. Stir-fry until the cabbage is wilted and the apples are softened. A nice side dish with a quick supper!

Easy Apple Ice Cream

1. Core, quarter, and peel four apples. Puree them in a food processor.
2. Add the following to the puree and blend in the food processor:

> 1/3 to 2/3 cup sugar (can increase to 1 cup for really tart apples)
> 2 cups heavy whipping cream or 1 cup cream and 1 cup sour cream (NOTE: you can substitute plain vanilla yogurt for the cream and sour cream, if desired)
> 1 tablespoon lemon juice
> 1/2 teaspoon cinnamon
> 1/4 teaspoon allspice
> 1/2 cup flaked coconut (optional)

3. Pour the mixture into your ice-cream maker and follow the manufacturer's instructions.

Easy Applesauce Ice

Superb plain, or with one of the seasonings!
1. Blend together:

> 2 cups applesauce
> 1/2 to 3/4 cup sugar
> 2 tablespoons lemon juice
> 1/2 teaspoon cinnamon and 1/4 teaspoon nutmeg or
> 2 teaspoons apricot brandy (both the spices and the brandy are optional)

2. Pour the mixture into your ice-cream maker and follow the manufacturer's instructions.

Easy Apple Ice

1. Core and quarter, but it's not necessary to peel, four apples.
2. Place the apples in a food processor and add:

> 1 1/2 cups apple juice (two 5.5 ounce cans).
> 3 or 4 tablespoons sugar
> 1 tablespoon lemon juice
> 1/8 teaspoon nutmeg (optional)

3. Puree until smooth. Place the mixture in your ice-cream maker and follow the manufacturer's instructions.

Easy Apple Sauce or Butter

I grew up helping my mother make this, and it's still a favorite!

FOR APPLE SAUCE, you need: apples and sugar to taste (I start with about 1/2 cup of sugar per 8 cups of apple quarters).

FOR APPLE BUTTER, you'll need additional sugar and spices to taste: cinnamon, nutmeg, and cloves in the following proportions:

For every 8 cups of apples, I add:

> 1 1/2 cups sugar
> 1 1/2 teaspoons cinnamon
> 3/4 teaspoon nutmeg
> 1/8 teaspoon cloves

HOW TO MAKE APPLE SAUCE OR APPLE BUTTER:

If you have a food mill or a vegetable strainer/food grinder attachment for your mixer, you can save a lot of time. When I make apple sauce or butter, I'm making huge batches, so I use the quickest method possible.

1. Wash the apples, remove any imperfections, and quarter them. I do not peel or core the apples, nor do I remove the stems.
2. Place the apple quarters in a big stainless steel kettle and add perhaps 1/2 inch of water.
3. Bring the apples to a boil; then reduce the heat to a medium simmer with the lid on, stirring occasionally.
4. When the apples are soft, remove them from the heat and run them through a food mill or your mixer's fruit strainer attachment. This removes the cores, seeds, stems, and skins, leaving apple puree.
5. Return the puree to the kettle, add the sugar for applesauce or the sugar and spices for apple butter, and continue simmering with the lid off until the sugar is dissolved and the batch is the right consistency for sauce or butter.

If you do not have a food mill or if you are doing smaller batches:

1. Prepare the apples by washing, peeling, quartering, and coring them.
2. Place the apples in a saucepan with a little water—perhaps 1/2 cup water per 8 cups of apples—and begin cooking, stirring often. You'll find the apples softening and falling apart rather soon.

3. Keep stirring until they're smooth or use a cordless hand blender right in the kettle.
4. For applesauce, add sugar and stir until it's dissolved. For apple butter, add the sugar and spices and continue simmering a few minutes longer, until the sugar is dissolved and the butter has thickened.

Cool the applesauce or apple butter and pour it into freezer containers, allowing a one-inch headspace for expansion. Label, date, and freeze.

Old-Fashioned Apple Pie

A classic farmer's wife's dessert!
1. Combine in a bowl:
> 7 cups sliced, peeled apples
> 1/2 to 3/4 cup sugar
> 2 tablespoons flour
> 3/4 teaspoon ground cinnamon

2. Pour fruit mixture into an unbaked pie shell.
3. Generously dot the filling with pats of butter. Sprinkle with additional cinnamon, if desired.
4. Top with crust and seal edges. Lightly sprinkle crust with sugar, if desired. Prick crust several times with a paring knife for ventilation.
5. Bake at 400 degrees F about 50 to 60 minutes or till crust is lightly browned and the apples are tender when a paring knife is inserted into the crust. Serve warm or cold as is, in a bowl topped with cream, or with a dollop of whipped cream or scoop of vanilla ice cream.

Great Apple Dumplings

A family favorite!
1. Roll out one recipe of pie crust into a square or rectangle. Cut into squares large enough to wrap around each apple.
2. Use six or eight apples, depending on size. Peel each apple and cut into the stem end to remove the core without cutting through the apple. Place apple on waxed paper. Put 1 teaspoon sugar, a dash of cinnamon, and a pat of butter inside each apple.

3. Place the apple upside down on the center of one pastry square. Remove waxed paper. Wrap the pastry around the apple, and seal. Right the apple and place it in a casserole dish large enough to hold all the dumplings. Repeat with all the apples. Sprinkle a little sugar on top of the dumplings.

4. In a saucepan, combine:

> 3/4 cup sugar
> 1 1/2 cups water
> 3 tablespoons butter
> 1/4 teaspoon cinnamon
> 1/4 teaspoon nutmeg

5. Bring just to a boil; then remove the saucepan from the stove.

6. Pour the liquid into the pan around the apple dumplings, being careful not to pour it directly over them.

7. Place the dumplings in the oven and bake at 375 degrees F for 45 minutes, or until the dumplings are lightly browned and the apples are tender. Serve each dumpling with some of the syrup.

Easy Baked Apples

The Farmer's favorite!

1. Use individual ovenproof serving dishes with lids, like Corningware's Grabbits. In each serving dish, place the following:

> 1 to 1 1/2 apples (I prefer Cortland), cored and sliced. (It's not necessary to peel the apples if they are home-raised using only organic sprays.) The thinner the apples are sliced, the quicker they will cook.
> 1 to 1 1/2 teaspoons lemon juice
> 1 teaspoon to 1 tablespoon brandy or cognac (optional).
> Ground cinnamon, up to 1/4 teaspoon per serving
> 1 teaspoon to 1 tablespoon of honey (the squirt-type bottle saves time and mess)
> 1 pat of butter (up to 1 tablespoon)
> Optional toppings: 1 tablespoon of raisins or shredded coconut or up to 2 tablespoons of coarsely chopped pecans or walnuts.

2. Cover each serving dish with a lid. Place the dishes on a cookie sheet or a cake pan. Bake in the oven at 350 degrees F until the apples are tender, about 30 minutes.

NOTE: This recipe cooks well in the microwave. If you don't have ovenproof lids, just use waxed paper or plastic wrap. Microwave on the "high" setting until the apples are tender, about five minutes for two servings.

3. Serve warm, topped with whipped cream or cinnamon whipped cream, vanilla ice cream, or milk.

Easy Apple Pudding

This old-fashioned recipe is tasty and quick to make!

1. Place 3 cups diced apples in the bottom of an 8 × 8-inch pan.
2. Sprinkle ⅓ cup sugar over the apples. Generously sprinkle with cinnamon.
3. Dice 4 slices of bread into cubes, drizzle with 2 tablespoons melted butter. Toss together. Place the bread cubes over the apples.
4. Bake at 350 degrees F for about 35 minutes. Serve with whipped cream.

Easy Applesauce Dessert

1. Combine:

    1 ½ cups applesauce
    1 cup sugar
    2 eggs
    1 teaspoon cinnamon
    ½ teaspoon nutmeg
    ⅛ teaspoon salt
    1 cup cream

2. Pour the filling into six or eight individual baking dishes or custard cups and place on a baking sheet or pan.
3. Bake at 400 degrees F for 15 minutes; then reduce the heat to 350 degrees F and bake another 30 to 35 minutes until done. Serve with a dollop of whipped cream, if desired.

APRICOTS IN THE GARDEN

The only way to enjoy the full flavor of this fabulous fruit is to pick it ripe off your very own tree. Store-bought apricots are harvested and shipped when they are still green because the fruit is hard and therefore less fragile, but, unfortunately, apricots do not increase their sugar content once they are picked.

There is one problem with growing your own apricots, however. Although some varieties can survive very cold winters, they bloom in early spring, one week before peaches, and their buds and blossoms are not tolerant of fluctuating temperatures and high wind. Another limitation: Some varieties can be harmed if the weather goes above 90 degrees F while the fruit is ripening.

Unfortunately, conditions are too harsh on our farm for apricot trees, although I've certainly tried! If you have a similar climate, one solution is to try the very hardy Manchurian bush apricots. Or consider growing dwarf apricots in wheeled containers that can be moved out of dangerous weather and overwintered in a cool building.

Description

Even better tasting than peaches, velvety soft apricots are smaller in size. The flesh can be orange, yellow, or creamy white. Apricots come in both tree and bush form.

Apricot trees are not shallow-rooted, but they tend to be short in stature and wide. Even the full-sized standards don't get much over fifteen feet tall, but the branches are spreading, sometimes up to twenty feet from the trunk.

LOCATION: Since apricots are small, think of planting a row or a grouping of at least two or three for design repetition and also for pollination. Although apricots will produce fruit on their own, planting another variety nearby increases the crop.

Don't plant apricots where they might be encouraged to bloom too early and risk getting nipped by frost, say against a wall that will warm in the winter sun, radiating heat to the tree.

If you live in a harsh climate, plant apricots where they won't get the brunt of winter.

GROWING RANGE: Many apricot trees prefer climates where the temperatures don't drop much below 0 degrees F, but there are now some hybrids that have been developed even to zone 3.

CHILL REQUIREMENT: Between 500 and 700 hours below 45 degrees F.

SOIL: Any deep, well-drained soil.

MOISTURE: Water the tree weekly if there hasn't been enough rain, especially in late-summer droughts. Dry weather causes the fruit to be small and mealy, and it also delays the tree's hardening for winter and might even cause winter-kill.

LIGHT: Full sun.

PLANTING SEASON: Spring.

HOW TO PLANT:
- Get reliable stock from a nursery.
- Follow the steps in the "Garden Notes" section for planting fruit trees.

PLANTING DISTANCE:
- Fifteen feet for dwarfs
- Thirty feet for standards

SUPPORT: None is needed unless the tree requires staking to withstand strong winds.

ONGOING CARE: In the early spring and throughout the summer, spray the trees with horticultural oil to combat insect problems.

PRUNING: Prune in early spring when training a young tree, or in summer for a mature tree. The idea is to shape the tree and also provide for sunlight to penetrate to the center. Heavy pruning will delay the production of fruit by several years.

WINTER PROTECTION: Take steps to prevent animals from damaging the trees.

VARIETIES INCLUDE:
- **Moorpark** has very large fruit with orange to almost brownish-red skin and juicy, sweet, bright orange flesh. The halves are often uneven. A hardy upright tree gets about ten feet tall. It may not set a large crop but it's worth growing because the fruit has excellent flavor and aroma. The fruit ripens at different times, which is an advantage to the home gardener. It's self-fruitful but produces better with Goldcot. Zones 4–8.
- **Goldcot** has medium fruit recommended for eating fresh or cooking. The tree gets to twenty feet tall and sets a large crop that might require thinning. Zones 4–9.
- **Royal** is the variety most popular in commercial orchards but the blossoms are very sensitive to temperature fluctuations. It produces a large fruit in big quantities but can't stand temperatures over 90 degrees while the fruit is ripening. Good fresh and cooked.
- **Sungold** and **Moongold** need each other for pollination. Both produce smaller fruit and are considered good for northern growers. Moongold has yellow-orange flesh and

orange skin that's rather tough. Its tree has a spreading habit with fruit that ripens in midsummer. Sungold has medium rounded fruit with a tender golden skin blushed orange; the tree is upright and the fruit ripens somewhat later than Moongold, a plus for home gardeners. Zones 4–8.

- **Garden Annie** is a self-fertile genetic dwarf, reaching only about six or seven feet in height. Its low chill requirement makes it a good container plant in the North. The fruit can be used fresh or cooked.
- **Goldenglo** is another genetic dwarf, growing only four to six feet tall. It starts bearing in the second year after planting. Zones 5–8.
- **Manchurian Bush Apricot** is, as the name implies, a ten- to twelve-foot shrub. The fruit is small but juicy and sweet. It's self-pollinating but produces better with two or more planted together. It is from Manchuria, where it withstands temperatures from –60 degrees F to 110 degrees F! Zones 2–9.

FRUITING: Apricots fruit in the second year, but there won't be a good crop until the third or fourth year. Most apricots are self-pollinating, but planting a second variety increases production.

Experts recommend thinning the fruit so that there is only one every three inches. This helps prevent the tree from falling into the cycle of bearing every other year and also increases winter hardiness since the tree is less depleted of energy.

YIELD: Apricots produce one to five bushels per season.

HARVESTING: Pick apricots when their color has changed to a rich orange without any green remaining. Another sign of ripeness is that the flesh will give when gently pressed.

If it's necessary, say when an early frost is on the way, you can pick the apricots partially green and ripen them in the house, although they won't be as good as tree-ripened. They can ripen on your countertop; to hasten the ripening process, place apricots in a closed paper bag. Once ripe, you can buy yourself a few more days by storing the apricots in the refrigerator. Place the apricots in a bowl or other container lined with a terry-cloth hand towel, and cover them with another towel—the towels will absorb moisture, which prevents the apricots from rotting, and the towels help protect the fruit from bruising. Never store apricots in a sealed plastic bag or container.

Apricots in the Kitchen

Harvesting apricots ripe from the tree will give you heavenly tasting fruit, but this means you must use them in fairly short order as they don't store well.

In addition, apricots tend to ripen all at once, so you will probably want a method of preserving your harvest. See the "Kitchen Notes" section for techniques for freezing pies, butters, etc. Or freeze apricots whole!

Freezing Apricots

DRY PACK: When they are ripe, place the whole fruit in a sealed plastic bag and freeze in a single layer, if possible. (I usually can get twenty-five apricots in a zipper bag, and these will stack nicely and conserve space in the freezer, once they are frozen solid.) Then label and date the bags.

When it's time to use them, lay the apricots in a single layer on the counter for about thirty minutes until partially thawed, and you can halve them and remove the pits. Now you can use the apricots as you would fresh fruit. Do remember to add a little more thickener (flour, corn starch, or tapioca) to the recipe if you use the frozen apricots for pies.

SUGAR PACK: Some people like to peel, pit, and slice the apricots and freeze them with sugar, using ⅔ cup sugar per quart of apricots. Be sure to note the sugar on the label.

OTHER: Apricot sauce, butter, and pies freeze well, also.

Eating Apricots

Home-grown apricots picked ripe and eaten fresh are outstanding! If you raise your own and do not use dangerous chemical sprays, just rinse them off and eat them with their skins on because skins are nutritious.

Serving Ideas

- Fresh apricots can be halved and topped with a dollop of whipped cream or cinnamon whipped cream.
- Fresh apricot halves can be sprinkled with a little sugar or honey to bring out their juice—this is the old farm technique that many still favor. Stir in a splash of apricot brandy, if desired.
- Apricot halves mixed with grapes, strawberries, kiwi, or other fruit make a delightful salad or dessert. Add a splash of lemon juice or apple juice to this mixture to keep the apricots from turning brown and provide a flavor jolt at the same time.
- Try tossing apricot halves with sliced pineapple and sweet red cherries.
- Combine diced fresh apricots with pineapple chunks and grapefruit or orange segments.
- Fresh sliced apricots are terrific topped with homemade vanilla or tapioca pudding. The pudding can be chilled or served still warm from the stove.

Easy Apricot Ice Cream

The apricot brandy is our favorite flavoring!
1. Puree pitted (but not skinned) apricots in a food processor to make 4 cups.
2. Add the following to the puree and blend in the food processor:

> 3/4 to 1 cup sugar (3/4 cup is good for apricots of average
>   sweetness)
> 1 cup heavy whipping cream

> 1/2 cup of half-and-half or sour cream (NOTE: You can substitute plain vanilla yogurt for the cream and half-and-half, if desired.)
>
> Juice of 1 lemon
>
> 2 tablespoons apricot brandy or 1 tablespoon amaretto or 3/4 teaspoon vanilla extract or 1/2 teaspoon grated fresh gingerroot

3. Pour the mixture into your ice-cream maker and follow the manufacturer's instructions.

Apricot Ice

1. Puree pitted but not peeled apricots in a food processor to make 4 cups.
2. Add and blend the following:

> the zest and juice of 1 lemon
>
> 2/3 to 1 1/3 cups sugar
>
> 1 cup apricot nectar, orange juice, or water
>
> 2 tablespoons apricot brandy (optional)

3. Pour the mixture into your ice-cream maker and follow the manufacturer's instructions. Or, if you don't have an ice-cream maker, put the mixture in your freezer in a metal bowl and remove it after 15 minutes and beat it well. Repeat this several times until it is firm enough to serve.

Apricot Sauce

The apricots freeze well in this sauce.

1. Place 3 cups of water and 3/4 to 1 cup sugar in a large saucepan and bring to a boil. Stir to dissolve the sugar.
2. Add the zest and juice of one lemon, one vanilla bean (optional), and 6 cups of apricot halves, with the skins on.
3. Turn the heat down and gently simmer, uncovered, until the apricots are tender, about 15 or 20 minutes.
4. Cool and serve. Or refrigerate or freeze with the vanilla bean, because it will continue to add flavor to the sauce.

Apricot Butter

1. Place 8 cups apricot halves, pitted but not peeled, in an open saucepan. (Or you can puree the apricots first and put the puree in the saucepan.)
2. Add the zest and juice of one orange or add ¾ cup apricot nectar. Bring the apricots to a boil and then reduce the heat to medium.
3. Stir in 6 cups of sugar.
4. Cook, uncovered, stirring often, until apricots and skins get tender and break up into an almost smooth sauce and are thickened into fruit butter, about 1 hour.
5. Use warm or chilled. Store in refrigerator or freeze.

Easy Apricot-Butter Dressing

1. Combine:

> 1 cup sour cream
> 1 cup apricot butter
> ½ cup flaked coconut
> ⅓ cup chopped walnuts

2. Serve with melon balls or on salads.

Broiled Apricots

Very quick and easy!
1. Halve and pit the apricots; there is no need to peel them.
2. Arrange the halves cut side up close together in an ovenproof pan.
3. Place one of the following on each half:

> a light sprinkling of mace
> grated lemon zest
> ⅛ teaspoon apricot brandy (our favorite!)
> ⅛ teaspoon cognac

4. Top each half with a thin pat of butter, probably less than ½ teaspoon.
5. If you like sweeter fruit, drizzle a few drops of honey on the apricots.
6. Broil on high about 3 inches from the heating element for 2 minutes. Serve.

Old-Fashioned Apricot Pie

1. Combine in a bowl:

> 5 cups pitted, but not peeled, apricots
> 1/2 to 3/4 cups sugar
> 1 teaspoon lemon juice
> 1/3 cup flour (if freezing the unbaked pie, increase to 6 or 7 tablespoons)
> 1/4 teaspoon cinnamon

2. Pour fruit mixture into an unbaked pie shell.
3. Generously dot the filling with pats of butter. Sprinkle generously with cinnamon, if desired.
4. Top with crust and seal the edges. Prick crust several times with a paring knife for ventilation. Lightly sprinkle crust with sugar, if desired.
5. Bake at 400 degrees F about 40 minutes or till crust is lightly browned and the apricots are tender when pricked with a paring knife. Serve warm or cold as is, or with a dollop of whipped cream or scoop of vanilla ice cream.

Easy Apricot Dessert

1. Melt 1/2 cup butter in a 2-quart baking pan in the microwave. Tip pan so butter coats the bottom.
2. Mix together in a bowl, then pour over the melted butter:

> 3/4 to 1 cup sugar
> 3/4 cup flour
> 3/4 cup cream
> 2 teaspoons baking powder

3. Mix together in a bowl, then pour over the batter:

> 2 cups pitted, but not peeled, apricots
> 1/4 to 1/2 cup sugar
> zest and juice of 1 lemon
> 1/4 teaspoon almond extract

4. Bake at 300 degrees F for 1 hour. The batter will rise to the top as it bakes. Serve as is or top with whipped cream or ice cream.

Sour Cream Apricot Dessert

This recipe uses six individual dessert dishes that are ovenproof and hold 1 to 1½ cups of liquid. Custard cups are too small for these servings.

1. Slice two pitted, but not skinned, apricots in the bottom of each dessert dish. Sprinkle a little lemon zest over the fruit (optional, but tasty!)
2. Mix together:

> ½ cup sugar
> ½ cup brown sugar, packed
> ¼ cup flour
> 1 cup sour cream

3. Pour a scant 1/3 cup of batter over each dish of apricot slices.
4. Bake for 30 minutes at 350 degrees F. Serve warm or cold.

BLACKBERRIES
IN THE GARDEN

Blackberries are a bush berry related to the raspberry, but the blackberry has larger fruit. The blackberry is shaped more like an upright bush than a sprawling thicket, and the canes can stand by themselves if properly pruned. Blackberries are one of my very favorite fruits!

Description

Blackberries are produced on the canes of a perennial shrub plant. Although traditionally full of thorns, newer varieties are thornless, very productive, and vigorous. When harvested, the white cores remain in the fruits, unlike raspberries, where the fruit cores remain on the plant.

LOCATION: When considering where to plant your blackberries, think in terms of hedges or groupings in the landscape. Blackberries form thickets that would be good along a fence or property line. Most blackberries are self-pollinating.

NOTE: Don't plant blackberries near raspberries or on ground where you've grown potatoes, tomatoes, eggplant, or peppers in recent years, as the soil may harbor verticillium wilt, preventing the canes from growing.

GROWING RANGE: The larger, sweeter hybrids are hardy to zone 5. Those living further north can grow the older, wilder types with thorns, which are dependable and very winter hardy, but have smaller, tarter fruit. In the far south, blackberries won't get the winter chill needed to set fruit, although a few varieties have been developed that don't require cool winters.

SOIL: Although blackberries can tolerate even poor soils, a deep sandy loam is preferred and accommodates the two- to three-foot root depth needed for maximum fruit production. If your soil is not the best, improve the harvest by tilling in organic material.

MOISTURE: Like most fruit, blackberries need ample moisture, especially when fruiting, but they don't want to be in soggy soil or standing water at any time. If you live in a wet area, consider planting your blackberries in raised beds to encourage drainage.

LIGHT: Blackberries must have full sun.

PLANTING SEASON: Plant blackberries in early spring, about one month prior to the last frost date for your area.

HOW TO PLANT:
- Purchase nursery plants that are twelve to fifteen inches tall, if possible, because they will take off faster.
- Till the planting bed thoroughly and deeply, mixing in plenty of well-rotted manure or compost, particularly if your soil is poor.
- Prune all the canes to six-inch stubs at planting.
- Plant the blackberries to the same depth as they grew in the nursery; do not allow the bright sun to shine on the bare roots.
- Space the blackberries about three to six feet apart in rows six to nine feet apart.

SUPPORT: The bushes are either upright or trailing, depending on the variety. The upright varieties produce the best harvest on arching, self-supporting canes about five feet tall.

The trailing varieties can be trained to an arbor or a fence. Some people use two poles set in the ground at either end of the blackberry row. Each pole has two crosspieces, one about knee height and one about shoulder height. Wire is strung to join opposite crosspieces, which looks like clotheslines. The canes can grow up loosely inside the wires or they can be attached to them with strips of pantyhose or cloth to give the canes support and to space them for maximum air and sun. Training also makes the harvest easier.

ONGOING CARE:

- Mulching increases the yield because it retains moisture and it will keep the weeds down so that you won't need to disturb the soil. You want to avoid cultivating around the plants because you'll risk damaging the underground suckers sent out to create the thicket, or you'll risk stimulating too much suckering.
- Dig out any suckers that appear where you don't want them to be. Don't merely prune these, because they can grow back again.
- Spraying the plants with horticultural (dormant) oil in very early spring will prevent insect problems.

PRUNING:

- Thin each plant back to four to six new canes per year.
- Prune the tips of new canes by about six inches, but not until they've reach thirty to forty inches tall. This encourages lateral branching and makes the canes stronger.
- Cut out all weak or dead wood. Blackberry canes live two years, producing fruit the second year. The canes are usually dead the third year, and if they aren't dead, they'll produce poorly. You should prune them out after they're done fruiting in the second year.
- Trim the canes as needed to allow you to walk among the bushes and to keep the growth from getting out of bounds.

NOTE: It's best to burn the canes you've pruned, to eliminate pests and disease.

POLLINATION: Although some hybrids are self-pollinating, most blackberries require bees for pollination. Be kind to both honeybees and bumblebees!

WINTER PROTECTION: In cold areas, mulch is essential to help the seedlings survive their first winter. Mulch insulates the plants from the cold and prevents them from breaking dormancy during winter warm spells, only to freeze again.

To "push" a warmer blackberry variety into living in a colder zone, some people dig a trench beside the bushes, bend the canes into the trenches, and cover them with several inches of soil to overwinter.

PROPAGATION: Suckers can be dug and replanted, if you are careful to get the roots, too. Do this within one month after the shoot leafs out in spring. Don't dig suckers that are growing within six inches of the plant base.

The longest year-old blackberry canes can be tipped to the ground and covered with a shovelful of soil from midsummer until fall. Leave them undisturbed all winter, and by the following spring the canes will be rooted. Cut the seedling free from the parent plant, dig it up, and you can start a new row. Incidently, you can also start a plant from a piece of root three inches or longer, planted in moist soil.

VARIETIES INCLUDE:

- **Darrow,** an excellent cold-hardy variety, that produces a heavy crop of extra large, juicy berries from mid- to late summer. The berries are great fresh or frozen and they bake well. This is the variety commonly carried by most nurseries. If you live in zone 5 to 10, or in zone 4 to –22 degrees F, I recommend that you try this wonderful blackberry!
- **Black Satin** is derived from Darrow to be thornless and has large flavorful berries in mid-July. It's self-pollinating, but you'll get more berries with a second variety nearby. A good choice for the Pacific Northwest and in zones 5–10.
- **Ebony King** originated in Michigan and has large, glossy black fruit that tastes very sweet and tangy. Good fresh, cooked, or frozen. Zones 5–9.

- **Eldorado** is a very hardy old variety that has fruit similar to Ebony King. Zones 4–9.

FRUITING: Harvest begins from one to three years after planting and often spans a two-month period. The fruit is formed on twiggy branches along the sides of canes that are one year old.

YIELD: From ten to twenty pounds per plant, depending on the variety and growing conditions.

HARVESTING: Blackberries are ready to harvest sometime in June or July, when they just begin to lose their shine, and they easily come off the cane. Once they begin to ripen, be sure to check the berries every day.

Blackberries are fragile, so handle them gently and place the fruit in a shallow container so the weight doesn't crush the lower berries.

NOTE: Blackberries stain clothing, so be certain to wear old or dark garments when collecting the ripe fruit.

Blackberries in the Kitchen

Refrigerate the blackberries after the harvest. Lay them in a shallow container lined with a paper towel if the quantity is small, or else use a dark-colored terry-cloth hand towel (so stains won't be a problem). Place another paper towel or terry towel on top. Never cover the blackberries with plastic wrap or seal berries in a plastic container with a lid because they will tend to spoil.

Do not wash berries before refrigerating them. Just give them a quick rinse in a colander just before you're ready to use them. Then place the berries on paper towels and gently pat them dry.

Freezing Blackberries

If the berries have not been sprayed, freeze them unwashed. Otherwise, rinse quickly in a colander and pat dry.

DRY PACK: For loose fruit, freeze the blackberries whole on paper-towel-lined baking sheets. When frozen solid, place the loose berries in a freezer bag or container, with as little air as possible. Seal, label, and freeze.

SUGAR PACK: Mix ⅔ cup sugar per quart of blackberries. Be sure to note the sugar on the label.

If you don't mind that the fruit is frozen into a solid block, you can pack the unfrozen berries in containers. Before serving or using the blackberries in a recipe, you can partially thaw the block and break up the fruit with a fork.

OTHER: Blackberries freeze well in pies, butters, sauce, etc.

Eating Blackberries

Fresh blackberries are among my favorite fruits. To eat them fresh, pick over the berries, removing any foreign matter. Place the berries in a colander and gently rinse them under cold water. Lay them out on a paper towel and lightly blot them dry.

Blackberries are delicious plain or served in a bowl with a little cream.

NOTE: Blackberries have seeds, so if eating these are a problem, run blackberries through a food mill either fresh, or after simmering them a short while in a very little water. This can be used as a puree in the recipes. Or press them through a double layer of cheesecloth.

Easy Blackberry Ice Cream

1. Puree blackberries in a food processor to make 4 cups. Remove seeds, if desired.
2. Add the following to the puree and blend in the food processor:

> 2/3 cups sugar (can increase to 1 cup, if preferred)
> 1 cup heavy whipping cream
> 1/2 cup half-and-half (NOTE: You can substitute plain vanilla yogurt for the cream and half-and-half, if desired.)
> 2 tablespoons frozen orange juice concentrate
> 2 tablespoons triple sec
> zest from one orange (optional)

3. Pour the mixture into your ice-cream maker and follow the manufacturer's instructions.

Easy Blackberry Ice

1. Puree blackberries in a food processor to make 3 cups. Strain to remove seeds, if desired.
2. Blend in ½ cup water and ¼ to ⅓ cup sugar.
3. Pour the mixture into your ice-cream maker and follow the manufacturer's instructions.

Blackberry Sauce or Butter

Place fresh blackberries in a saucepan. Add just a little water—enough to coat the bottom until the fruit juice is released. Add ¾ to 1½ cups of sugar and 2 tablespoons of lemon juice or orange juice per 4 or 5 cups of blackberries. If desired, stir in 1 teaspoon of cinnamon or a little minced gingerroot. Simmer a few minutes for sauce, or a few minutes longer until thickened for fruit butter. Store in the refrigerator or freeze.

Old-Fashioned Blackberry Pie

1. Place 4 cups fresh whole blackberries in the bottom of an unbaked pie shell.
2. Combine the following and pour over the berries:

> I cup heavy whipping cream
> 2/3 cup sugar (increase to I cup, if preferred)
> 1/4 cup flour
> 1/2 teaspoon cinnamon
> pinch salt

3. Generously dot the filling with pats of butter.
4. Top with crust and seal edges. Lightly sprinkle crust with sugar, if desired. Prick crust several times with a paring knife for ventilation.
5. Bake at 400 degrees F about 35 minutes or till crust is lightly browned.
6. Serve as is or topped with cream, a dollop of whipped cream, or a scoop of vanilla ice cream.

Stovetop Blackberry Dumplings

Very quick and easy! Although this will serve eight, you can halve the recipe in a medium saucepan for four servings.

1. To make dumplings, combine the following in a medium bowl:

> I cup flour
> 1/4 cup sugar
> 2 teaspoons baking powder
> 1/2 teaspoon salt
> 3/4 cup cream or milk

2. To make the sauce, combine the following in a large saucepan:

> 4 cups blackberries
> 1/3 to 2/3 cup sugar
> 1 1/3 cup water
> I tablespoon lemon juice
> 1/4 teaspoon ground nutmeg

3. Bring the blackberries to a boil; then reduce to medium heat.

4. Drop one eighth of the dumpling batter into a different area of the blackberry sauce. Cover the pan with a lid and cook for 10 to 12 minutes.

5. Remove the pan from the burner. Serve the dumplings with a generous portion of the blackberry sauce, warm or cold. Top with whipping cream, if desired.

Sour Cream Blackberry Dessert

This recipe uses six individual dessert dishes that are ovenproof and hold 1 to 1½ cups of liquid. Custard cups are too small for these servings.

1. Place ¼ to ¾ cup whole blackberries in the bottom of each dessert dish. Sprinkle with a little lemon zest (optional, but tasty!).

2. Mix together:

> ½ cup sugar
> ½ cup brown sugar, packed
> ¼ cup flour
> 1 cup sour cream

3. Pour a scant ⅓ cup of batter over each dish of blackberries.

4. Bake for 30 minutes at 350 degrees F. Serve warm or cold.

BLUEBERRIES IN THE GARDEN

A lovely ornamental shrub, the blueberry is covered in blossoms in the spring and decorative fruit in the summer. Blueberries are easy to grow and take little care. They can be raised anywhere so long as they can get some winter chill and the proper soil conditions.

The most important thing to remember about growing blueberries is that, unlike most other fruit, they require an acid soil with a pH of 4.8 to 5.0. If you can grow azaleas and rhododendrons in your soil, you can grow blueberries without doing anything special. Everyone else will have to amend their soil to create the acid condition required—which is not difficult, but does take consistent effort, more than other fruits.

Description

Blueberries grow on perennial shrubs. Blueberry varieties suitable for the southern areas, the rabbit-eyes, are often ten to twelve feet tall. Those suited to the northern climates, the highbush blueberries, usually are smaller, from two to six feet in height.

LOCATION: Combine blueberries in the landscape with other acid-loving shrubs, like azaleas and rhododendrons. Plant the blueberries closer than recommended if you want a hedge.

GROWING RANGE: The highbush varieties grow over most of the United States except for the Deep South, where the rabbit-eye varieties do well. Do not plant blueberries in areas with limestone.

CHILL REQUIREMENT: The highbush varieties must have a long winter chill of seven hundred to eight hundred hours; the rabbit-eye varieties are low- or no-chill.

SOIL: Acid soil that is light and well drained. Blueberries like a lot of moisture but do not want to stand in soggy soil that drowns and rots the roots. This means that they don't do well in heavy clay-type soils, which their roots can't penetrate easily, and which do not allow for aeration. Add sand and lots of peat to clay soil for blueberries.

How to get acid soil:

Some gardeners mix oak or maple leaves and pine needles into the planting soil; others use wood chips and pine bark. I recommend using peat moss. Mix the soil with equal parts of peat moss (or increase to three-quarters peat moss for heavy soils). The peat increases drainage, makes the soil light, and adds acid. A gardener friend swears that throwing a few rusty nails into the planting hole will provide the acid condition needed for blueberries, though I haven't tried this yet.

This is one plant that should not be fertilized with rotted manure because it will upset the acid balance. Use ammonium sulfate by mixing about two tablespoons into the soil at planting time and another tablespoon every spring, summer, and fall per plant to maintain acidity. Increase this amount to ¼ cup per bush when they reach full maturity.

MOISTURE: Keep the soil moist but not soggy. Water frequently to keep the soil moist to one inch, where the roots are. Drip irrigation or overhead sprinkling systems work well.

If there is any chance of standing water, plant the blueberries in raised beds for drainage.

LIGHT: Full sun.

PLANTING SEASON: Spring in most areas; spring or fall in the Deep South.

HOW TO PLANT:

- Start with two-year-old nursery plants.
- Do not prune highbush varieties; do prune rabbit-eyes back to four to six inches at planting.
- Till the soil thoroughly to eight inches deep and at least two feet wide per plant, and mix in peat or sand, as needed.
- Plant the bush so that the roots are spread out and shallow, one inch below the surface. Spread the roots out gently, never bunch them up or squeeze them into a small hole.
- Do not allow the roots to dry out in planting or beyond. They don't have root hairs and rely on a fungus that helps the roots absorb nutrients; this fungus will die if it dries out.
- The young blueberry roots need a wide area of loose soil to get established, so be sure you don't tamp it down or step on it.
- For highbush varieties: space the bushes four to six feet apart in rows ten feet apart.
- For rabbit-eye varieties: space the bushes five or six feet apart in rows ten to twelve feet apart.
- Water the new planting with an acid fertilizer for azaleas (not aluminum sulfate).
- Cover the area with mulch to hold in moisture. Sawdust is ideal, but it robs the soil of nitrogen, so add one pound of ammonium sulfate per bushel of sawdust.

SUPPORT: None needed.

ONGOING CARE:

- Maintain mulch at three to six inches deep, using acid plant material like peat moss, pine needles, sawdust, etc. Mulch holds in moisture, keeps the weeds down, and helps the plant to overwinter.
- Blueberries are shallow-rooted, so do not dig or hoe around

the bushes; mulch will keep the weeds down.
- Remove all the blossoms the first year, to help the plant get established.
- Protect the fruit from birds.

PRUNING:
- Remove dead or broken canes.
- Let them grow for two or three years without pruning, except to remove damaged or tangled branches.
- In the early spring after the third year, during dormancy, prune out the older canes as they will produce only a few small berries. Each crown should have six to ten canes upon maturity. More than this number reduces the berry size; less increases it.
- Sometimes the new canes grow vigorously and are much taller than the older canes; just trim them back to match the average height of the older canes to keep the shrub shapely.

POLLINATION: Planting more than one variety will increase yields.

WINTER PROTECTION: Snow piled against the bushes insulates them from cold in below-zero winters, in addition to a thicker layer of mulch for winter.

PROPAGATION: Stem cuttings.

VARIETIES INCLUDE:
- **Bluecrop**, which ripens mid-July. The berries are huge, light blue, and rather tart. The fruit stores well and cooks well. Vigorous grower. Zones 3–7.
- **Patriot** matures its fruit in July. Large, rather flat berries on bushes five to seven feet tall. Resists root rot. Two to five pounds fruit per plant per year. Zones 3–7.
- **Jersey,** which grows five to seven feet tall. The fruit ripens in late July and is good to freeze. Zones 3–8.
- **Northblue** grows two feet tall, matures in mid-June, and yields two to five pounds of fruit. Berries are quite large. Zones 4–7.

- **Northsky** grows eighteen inches tall and two to three feet wide, and yields one to two pounds of small to medium sky-blue fruit yearly. It can withstand temperatures to –40 degrees F with snow cover. Zones 3–7.
- **Dwarf Tophat** stays small at twenty inches tall and two feet wide, but the fruit remains large. A good container plant and good for an ornamental bush. Zones 4–10.
- **Tiftblue**, the most popular rabbit-eye variety, grows into a vigorous upright bush eight to fourteen feet tall. It is the most cold-hardy of the rabbit-eyes. Pollinate with Woodward. Zones 7–9.
- **Woodward**, a rabbit-eye variety, has an excellent flavor. Pollinate with Tiftblue. Zones 7–9.

NOTE: If you don't want to fuss with making your soil acid, you might consider planting the Saskatoon Blueberry, which isn't really a blueberry although it tastes like one. It's hardy nearly everywhere, at least zones 2 through 8, although one source claims it's hardy to –60 degrees F. The berries are ready in July. One variety grows to eight feet tall and another grows to fifteen to twenty feet tall. Both are self-pollinating and have masses of white flowers. These are actually june berries or service berries and were used by Native Americans to pound into wild meat and fat to make pemmican.

FRUITING: Remove all the flowers the first year, to focus the plant's energies on getting the roots established. You'll get a crop in the second season, usually in June and July, and it can last over a six-week period.

YIELD: Highbush varieties produce four to eight or more pints per plant; rabbit-eye varieties produce up to thirty pints.

HARVESTING: Ripe blueberries are plump and firm, and the fruit should have no dimples or dents. The skin should be dull, almost dusty-looking. They are ready for harvest in midsummer when they easily fall off the cane. Always taste the berries before you start to harvest them; they can look ripe when they are still quite tart.

Blueberries in the Kitchen

Refrigerate the berries right away after picking them, lining the container with paper towels or dark terry cloth. Cover the berries with more paper towels or terry cloth, never use plastic wrap or seal them in a plastic container.

Quickly rinse blueberries just before they are needed; do not soak them in water as you will lose fruit juices.

NOTE: Always keep in mind that blueberries can stain clothing; when cooking with blueberries or washing dishes you've used for them, dress appropriately.

Freezing Blueberries

DRY PACK: Blueberries should be frozen without washing them first. Lay the fruit out in a single layer on baking sheets. When frozen, seal the fruit in freezer bags or containers, label, and return to the freezer.

SUGAR PACK: Mix ⅔ cup sugar per quart of blueberries. Be sure to note the addition of sugar on the label.

Quickly rinse the frozen berries in a colander just before use.

OTHER: Blueberry butter, sauce, and pies freeze well.

Eating Blueberries

Easy Blueberry Ice Cream

Absolutely superb—you must try this one!

1. Place 2 cups of blueberries in a food processor and puree them.
2. Add the following to the puree and blend in the food processor:

> ⅔ cup sugar (can increase to 1 cup, if preferred)
> 1 cup heavy whipping cream
> 1 cup sour cream (NOTE: You can substitute plain or
> vanilla yogurt for the cream and sour cream, if desired.)

> 2 tablespoons dark rum or 1 1/2 teaspoons vanilla (Both
> taste wonderful, but we highly recommend the rum.)

3. Pour the mixture into your ice-cream maker and follow the manufacturer's instructions.

Easy Blueberry Ice

1. Place 2 cups of blueberries in a food processor and puree them.
2. Add the following to the puree and blend in the food processor:

> 1/2 to 1 cup sugar
> 1 cup water
> 1 tablespoon lemon juice
> 1/2 teaspoon vanilla

3. Pour the mixture into your ice-cream maker and follow the manufacturer's instructions.

Blueberry Sauce or Butter

Place fresh blueberries in a saucepan. Add just a little water—enough to coat the bottom until the fruit juice is released. Add 1 to 2 cups of sugar and 4 or 5 tablespoons of lemon juice per gallon of blueberries. Simmer a few minutes for sauce, or a few minutes longer until thickened for fruit butter. Store in the refrigerator or freeze.

Old-Fashioned Blueberry Pie

1. Mix together in a bowl:

> 4 cups blueberries
> 2/3 to 1 cup sugar
> 1/3 cup flour
> 1 tablespoon lemon juice

2. Place blueberry mixture in an unbaked pie shell and dot liberally with butter. Sprinkle with cinnamon, if desired.
3. Top with crust and seal the edges. Prick crust several times with a paring knife for ventilation. Lightly sprinkle crust with sugar, if desired.
4. Bake at 400 degrees F about 40 minutes or till crust is lightly

browned. Serve warm or cold as is, or with a dollop of whipped cream or scoop of vanilla or cinnamon ice cream.

Dutch Blueberry Pie

Follow directions for the Old-Fashioned Blueberry Pie, above, except pour ½ cup heavy cream over the blueberry filling before topping with the crust.

Stovetop Blueberry Dumplings

Very quick and easy! Although this will serve eight, you can halve the recipe in a medium saucepan for four servings.

1. To make dumplings, combine the following in a medium bowl:

> 1 cup flour
> ¼ cup sugar
> 2 teaspoons baking powder
> ½ teaspoon salt
> ¾ cup cream or milk

2. To make the sauce, combine the following in a large saucepan:

> 4 cups blueberries
> ⅓ to ⅔ cup sugar
> 1 ⅓ cup water
> 1 tablespoon lemon juice
> ¼ teaspoon ground nutmeg

3. Bring the blueberries to a boil; then reduce to medium heat.
4. Drop one-eighth of the dumpling batter into a different area of the blueberry sauce. Cover the pan with a lid and cook for 10 to 12 minutes.
5. Remove the pan from the burner. Serve the dumplings with a generous portion of the blueberry sauce, warm or cold. Top with whipping cream, if desired.

CANTALOUPE IN THE GARDEN

We can hardly wait until late summer when the cantaloupe get ripe—let the feasting begin! Unlike most fruits and berries, cantaloupe are annuals that must be planted every year from seed. The fruits are almost the size of basketballs and have a delectable aroma and flavor. Even if you don't have a patch for melons, you can incorporate them into the landscape. They are well worth the effort!

The most important thing to remember about cantaloupe is that they like heat. The soil must be warm before the seeds will even germinate, and the plants prefer weather in the 80-degree-F range and above—and do well even over 100 degrees F! They are the last seeds I plant in the spring, and I delay planting until late May or even June if we aren't having warm, sunny days.

The other thing to keep in mind about cantaloupe is that although they need moisture, they absolutely can't tolerate soggy soil or standing water. You must plant them in an area where they'll have good drainage. A sandy hill would be perfect, or you can add some sand to your soil to increase drainage. Another possibility is to use raised beds, which would be lovely incorporated into the landscape with cement stone edging; or a quick, inexpensive method is to lay down an old tire filled with dirt in your backyard. After the soil is well warmed, mulching will keep the weeds down and moisture off the plant and the fruit. Don't let the fruit come into contact with moist ground or mulch that stays damp, or it will rot and become wormy. I elevate each fruit by placing it on a board or cement stone.

Description

Cantaloupes are an annual vine that must be planted outside after the soil is warm and all danger of frost is past.

LOCATION: Rotate the planting ground, starting cantaloupe in a new location each spring. Be sure you choose a site where you haven't grown cucumbers, squash, or pumpkins for three years, to avoid insect and disease problems.

Many gardeners give cantaloupe their own patch, or they incorporate cantaloupes in their vegetable or flower garden. If space is short, you can choose compact vines that take only three or three and a half feet, or consider training cantaloupe vines on a trellis. (See "Support," below.)

GROWING RANGE: Nearly everywhere, with a few adjustments; for example, watering in dry climates, using black plastic to warm the soil in very cold climates, etc.

CHILL REQUIREMENT: None—frost kills cantaloupes.

SOIL: Cantaloupes prefer light, fertile soil, so in addition to adding sand for drainage, add a good measure of well-rotted manure or compost for nutrients and aeration.

MOISTURE: Cantaloupes need adequate moisture during the entire growing season, at least one inch of water per week, so you'll need to hand-water if nature doesn't cooperate. Be sure the plants get continuous moisture during flowering and fruit formation.

The water should be directed only at the roots; to avoid disease, be careful not splash water onto the plant.

LIGHT: Full sun.

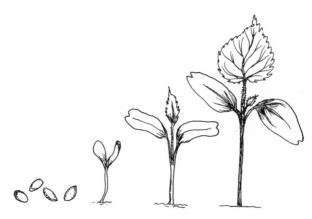

PLANTING SEASON: Two weeks after the last frost date for your area.

HOW TO PLANT:

- You can start cantaloupe seedlings indoors two weeks prior to the last frost date for your area, and then transplant them when they are about one month old, when the weather is consistently warm. If the seedlings go outside into cool weather, they will die—so don't put them out too soon. Plant two or three seeds per pot, and then snip off all but the best one. It's best to use peat pots that can be placed directly into the ground without disturbing the roots. Grow the seedlings in a bright, sunny window or under a light stand (see "Sources").

Light stand

- Thoroughly till the entire planting area, adding in well-rotted manure, compost, or sand if needed.
- To make watering easier, you can bury a one-gallon plastic milk jug that has had holes punched into it, so that only the neck shows. Then plant the seeds in a circle around the milk jug. To water, just fill the jug with a hose or watering can once or twice a week, or as needed. The water will drip out at the root system.
- If direct planting, wait until the soil is warm and the weather is well past any sign of frost. Plant six seeds together in a

hill cluster, spacing the seeds three inches from each other and the hills at least four feet apart.

- Cover the seeds with half an inch to an inch of fine soil and firm lightly.
- Keep the seeds evenly moist and they'll sprout in one or two weeks.
- After the seedlings are two or three inches high, pinch off—don't pull—about half the plants, leaving the most vigorous ones. If you are using a car tire as a planter, allow only two seedlings to grow; a large tractor tire can support four or five plants.

SUPPORT: Cantaloupes will grow without support, although some gardeners train them to a trellis to conserve garden space. I like to use steel cattle panel fencing, available at farm and ranch supply stores, which can be shaped to form A-frames.

The trellis must be sturdy because the fruit and vines are heavy. Use something soft to tie up the vines, like cloth or, best of all, pantyhose. You'll need to support the fruit with 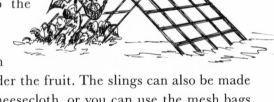 slings tied to the trellis under the fruit. The slings can also be made of recycled pantyhose or cheesecloth, or you can use the mesh bags that you get when buying onions or potatoes. The idea is to allow the air to circulate and moisture to quickly evaporate.

In addition to saving space, trellising cantaloupes is the very best way to prevent insect or disease problems, which come when the vine is on the ground and in contact with the soil, particularly moist soil. For this reason, trellising is the best choice for rainy climates.

ONGOING CARE:

- Fertilize: If you don't have rotted manure for fertilizer, seaweed emulsion is great. Apply it according to directions at planting, at fruit set, and two weeks after fruit set.
- Allow the vines to grow naturally, radiating out from the hills, gently turning them if they should go beyond their des-

ignated area. To conserve space, you can train them to spiral around the plant hills, but don't place them so close that the vines or leaves are touching. They need ample room for air circulation and plenty of sunshine.

- You can enhance the flavor of your cantaloupes if you stop watering about two weeks before harvest. The cantaloupe is encouraged to concentrate sugar into the fruit, rather than enlarging the fruit size. Also, in fall, removing all the blossoms and the really young fruit that can't live long enough to mature will encourage the development of the remaining fruit and also enhance the flavor.

PRUNING: None until fall, when you might want to prune the vine tips to encourage the existing fruit to mature.

POLLINATION: Some cantaloupes are self-pollinating, and some have both male and female flowers on the same plant and must be pollinated by bees.

PROPAGATION: By seed.

WINTER PROTECTION: As annuals, cantaloupes do not survive winter.

VARIETIES INCLUDE:
- **Hybrid Ambrosia**, so aptly named; this one is my personal favorite! It has medium-sized fruit with peach-colored flesh that is extra sweet and mouth-watering good right down to the rind. Eighty-six days to maturity.
- **Hale's Best Jumbo** is drought-tolerant yet produces large, high-quality, sweet fruit in ninety days.
- **Hybrid Alaska** is the choice for areas with short summers. Each vine yields four or five sweet fruits that mature quickly. Sixty-five days to maturity.
- **Minnesota Midget** has compact vines only three to three and a half feet long. Smaller, sweet fruit are early to ripen and produce a good crop in a limited space. Sixty-five days to maturity.

• **Short and Sweet** is a compact, nonvining variety that is ready in seventy days.

FRUITING: The fruit will start to ripen about thirty-five to forty-five days after pollination.

YIELD: Two to eight cantaloupes per vine, depending on variety and growing conditions.

HARVESTING: Cantaloupes are ripe when the stem separates easily from the fruit—sometimes you can see a crack where the fruit has started to separate on its own. The netting on the rind should be thick and close, and the spaces between the netting should be yellow or yellow-green.

Very ripe melons release an aroma that is attractive not only to humans, but to insects as well. Check the fruit daily as it gets close to maturity, so that you pick it before it's overripe and full of bugs. If insects have attacked only a small area, just cut it off and you can eat the rest of the fruit.

When the night temperature stays in the 50-degree-F range or less, the vines shut down and the unripe cantaloupes won't take on more sugar or ripen. When the temperature drops to freezing, the vines will die and collapse right away.

When frost is possible, harvest all the fruits that are nearly mature, and finish ripening them in the house. They won't have the same wonderful flavor as vine-ripened cantaloupes, but they're still worth eating.

Cantaloupe in the Kitchen

It's best to harvest the cantaloupe fully ripened, but if you can't, or if you're bringing in the last of the harvest a little green due to impending frost, you can ripen a cantaloupe in a brown paper bag.

Ripe cantaloupe smells wonderful, but it can flavor the other foods in your refrigerator. When you chill the whole cantaloupe, seal it in a plastic bag or container. It will keep in the refrigerator a week or two, sometimes more.

Freezing Cantaloupe

DRY PACK: Remove the seeds and peel and slice the cantaloupe into one-inch cubes. Pack into freezer containers. Seal, label, and freeze.
   Serve partially frozen or else make it into ice cream or ice.

Eating Cantaloupe

Cantaloupe is wonderful fresh from the garden. First wash and dry the whole fruit; then cut off segments and remove the seeds with a spoon or your fingers and serve it in the rind. (The rind is not eaten.)

Serving Ideas

- For a variation, serve the fresh cantaloupe wedges with a squeeze of fresh lemon juice.
- Cut the rind off the segments, cut the segments into chunks, and serve chilled. Be sure to store in a covered container.
- Halve or quarter cantaloupe, removing the seeds. Top each half or quarter with a dollop of whipped cream, yogurt, or vanilla ice cream. Then sprinkle fresh berries or grapes on top, if desired. So simple, pretty, and delicious!
- Toss cantaloupe chunks with coconut for an attractive salad.
- Cantaloupe halves or quarters can be used as serving bowls for chicken or tuna salad.
- Cantaloupe Pecan Salad: Put cantaloupe balls on top of lettuce and combine the following for a topping: 3 ounces cream cheese, ¼ cup mayonnaise, ¼ cup minced celery, 2 tablespoons chopped pecans. When mixed well, fold in ½ cup whipped cream.
- Serve cantaloupe with whole or chopped fresh mint leaves for a refreshing dessert.

Easy Cantaloupe Ice Cream

Wonderful!

1. Puree cantaloupe to make 3 cups.
2. Add 1 cup cream and 1 teaspoon vanilla or 2 tablespoons brandy.
3. Pour the mixture into your ice-cream maker and follow the manufacturer's instructions.
4. If desired, serve with a sprinkle of ground ginger or ground cinnamon.

NOTE: There is no need for added sugar if the cantaloupe is ripe and sweet.

Easy Cantaloupe Ice

Perfect on a hot summer day!

NOTE: Cantaloupe puree can be made into ice without adding any other ingredients—just put 4 cups puree (or the amount desired) into your ice-cream maker and follow the manufacturer's instructions. If your cantaloupe isn't flavorful and juicy, you might want to try the following recipe:

1. Puree cantaloupe chunks in a food processor to make 3½ cups.
2. Blend into the cantaloupe:

> 1/4 cup lemon juice or orange juice
> 1/4 to 1/2 cup sugar
> 1/2 cup water

3. Pour the mixture in your ice-cream maker and follow manufacturer's instructions.

NOTE: You can substitute peach puree for part of the cantaloupe, if desired.

Easy Cantaloupe Butter

1. Combine in a kettle:

> 6 cups cantaloupe puree (1 large cantaloupe)
> 2 to 2½ cups sugar
> juice of 1 lemon
> 3 tablespoons quick-cooking tapioca

2. Heat till it comes to a full boil. Reduce heat and continue boiling for five minutes. Remove from the heat and cool. The butter will thicken as it cools. Pour into containers and refrigerate or freeze.

Cantaloupe Fruit Butter

Combine in a saucepan the flesh of one cantaloupe, two peeled and chopped oranges, and six cut-up peaches. Simmer in a small amount of water for ten minutes or until soft. Using a cordless hand blender or a food processor, puree the fruit. Stir in between ½ to 1 cup of sugar per each cup of puree. Return to the saucepan and simmer for one hour. Cool and serve or pour into freezer containers. Seal, label and date, and freeze.

Very Easy Cantaloupe Pie

1. Empty one 3-ounce package of peach gelatin into a small bowl. Pour ½ cup of boiling water over the gelatin and stir until it's dissolved. Set aside.
2. Puree cantaloupe to make 3 cups (one average-size melon).
3. Return part of the puree back to the food processor and blend it with 3 ounces of cream cheese. Add the remaining cantaloupe and the gelatin and blend thoroughly.
4. Pour the mixture into a prepared and baked pastry shell or graham cracker crust. Chill thoroughly in the refrigerator.
5. Serve very cold. If your refrigerator isn't cold enough, chill the pie in the freezer until almost frozen, about 30 minutes. Serve with whipped cream, and garnish with a mint leaf, if desired.

Cooked Cantaloupe Pudding or Pie Filling

1. Combine in a saucepan:

> 1 ½ cups sugar
> ¼ cup flour

2. Add 5 eggs and mix well.
3. Stir in 1½ cups cantaloupe puree. Cook on medium heat, stirring

constantly. Do not be tempted to hurry the cooking with a higher heat setting. The mixture will thicken. When it starts to bubble, continue cooking it for one more minute.

4. Take the pudding off the heat and stir in 3 tablespoons of butter and 1½ teaspoons vanilla.

5. As pudding, serve it warm or cold, topped with whipped cream, if desired. As a pie filling, put it in a baked pastry or graham cracker crust and chill. Whip 1 cup of cream and spread on top of the pie. Serve cold.

Easy Cantaloupe Salad

To make the dressing, combine 1 cup of mayonnaise with ⅓ cup orange juice concentrate. Serve cantaloupe slices or halves on a lettuce leaf. Place fruit or fruit mixtures like blueberries, grapes, strawberries, and peaches on top of the cantaloupe. Spoon the dressing over all and serve.

Easy Cantaloupe Soup

Refreshing!

1. Puree cantaloupe to make 3 cups.
2. Add:

> 1 cup heavy cream or substitute plain yogurt
> ¼ cup apricot brandy
> ¼ cup honey (optional)
> ¾ teaspoon ground ginger or cinnamon or dried mint

3. Serve well chilled.

CHERRIES IN THE GARDEN

Few sights can beat the breathtaking beauty of a blooming cherry tree; the vast number of blossoms required to produce a crop of the small fruits almost covers every inch of the tree in early spring. The flowers on our tart cherry trees give way to loads of bright red fruit that have a luminous glow in the early morning sun. I have fond memories of my grandfather's cherry tree as I grew up, and even fonder memories of the pies and other treats my mother made from it!

Description

SWEET CHERRIES are the kind you can buy fresh in stores. The fruit can be deep red, white, or even golden in color, and it is larger than the sour cherry. Sweet cherry trees require winter chill but can't survive in the cold northern winters.

Most sweet cherry tree varieties are standard height, although some dwarfs are available. Standards can grow quite tall, over thirty-five feet, and serve as a shade tree; dwarfs reach only fifteen or twenty feet, and genetic dwarfs are shorter yet.

SOUR CHERRIES or "pie" cherries are often preferred for cooking. They are not available fresh in stores, but they are available canned and are traditionally used in canned pie filling. The fruit has red skin and yellow flesh. Sour cherry trees can grow almost everywhere and tolerate extremes of heat and cold. Sour cherries are self-pollinating, so you can get by with only one tree, and they are beautiful in bloom.

Most standard-size sour cherry trees grow up to twenty feet, dwarfs up to fifteen feet, and there are some genetic dwarfs that are about half that height.

BUSH CHERRIES can be planted in the ground or adapted to container growth. The fruit is good eaten fresh and it makes great pies and cherry butter.

LOCATION: Don't plant cherries where peaches or cherries grew previously. Plant cherries where they'll receive some protection if you live in a windy area or in a climate that might get too cold for sweet cherries.

Sour cherries are self-fertile, so you can get by planting only one tree. Many sweet cherries do better with at least one other compatible variety nearby to increase pollination, but there are self-fertile varieties and you can buy two types grafted onto one tree.

If space is a problem, even for genetic dwarf-sized trees, consider bush cherries. They can be planted as a hedge and will withstand pruning and shearing. Cherries can be espaliered.

Bush cherries can be container-grown, but they will need winter chill, depending on the variety.

GROWING RANGE: Sweet cherries prefer a milder climate no colder than zone 5. Sour cherries are very hardy, to zone 3 and even zone 2, and yet some varieties can still take the heat through zone 8. They don't like the long, hot summers of the South unless at higher altitudes.

CHILL REQUIREMENT: Sour cherries need at least 1,000 hours below 45 degrees F in the winter; sweet cherries need about 700 hours.

SOIL: All cherries like rich soil at least four feet deep. They will grow in shallow soil, but their production will be lowered.

MOISTURE: Cherries need plenty of moisture, but don't want to be standing in water.

LIGHT: Plant cherries in full sun; they will tolerate partial shade, but the fruit yield will be reduced.

PLANTING SEASON: Spring.

HOW TO PLANT:
- Select nursery stock appropriate for your area.
- Plant the trees the same depth as they grew in the nursery.
- Follow general tree planting instructions in the "Garden Notes" section.
- For sweet cherries: Space standards thirty to thirty-five feet apart and dwarfs about ten feet apart.
- For sour cherries: Space standard trees fifteen feet apart and dwarfs eight feet apart.
- For bush cherries: space the plants four or more feet apart, depending on variety.

SUPPORT: Not required except for staking new trees in windy areas.

ONGOING CARE: Spraying with horticultural oil in the early spring for sour cherries, and throughout the summer for sweet cherries, to combat insect problems.

If you live in a dry area, a thick mulch the width of the tree top will help retain moisture.

PRUNING: Sweet and sour cherries need less pruning than many fruits. My sour cherry trees have produced heavily without much pruning. As necessary, remove any dead or crossed branches, and thin out the tree a bit to let in air and light.

If you live in a windy area, be sure to remove branches that aren't upright enough, because these are vulnerable to breaking off and splitting the tree. I've lost several sour cherry trees that toppled in high winds, including one the spring I'm writing this.

POLLINATION: Most sweet cherries require cross-pollination; plant at least one other variety. Sour cherries are self-pollinating.

WINTER PROTECTION: None. If your winters are severe, plant them where they'll have protection from harsh winds.

PROPAGATION: Cherry trees can be started from the seeds in the fruit, or, when the fruit is ripe, from softwood cuttings that are dipped in hormone powder and planted in soil. A grafted tree develops a taproot that enables it to withstand drought; plants grown from cuttings don't develop taproots and are less able to withstand drought.

VARIETIES INCLUDE:
Sweet Cherries

- **Bing**, a favorite sweet cherry that has fruit that is extra large, heart-shaped, and deep mahogany red to almost black in color. In humid climates, this variety is subject to bacterial leaf spot. Needs a pollinator. Zones 5–8.
- **Garden Bing** is a genetic dwarf that grows up to eight feet tall and is suitable for containers, where it grows only a few feet tall. It has the dark red Bing fruit and is self-pollinating. Zones 5–8.
- **Black Tartarian** also has extra large, very sweet fruit that is dark red to purplish-black in color on a twenty-five- to thirty-foot-tall tree. Needs a pollinator. Zones 5–7.
- **Compact Stella** is a genetic dwarf that gets only seven to nine feet tall. The tree is productive and self-fruitful. The fruit is large, dark red to black, and heart-shaped. A good pollinator for other sweet cherries. Zones 5–9.

Sour Cherries

- **Montmorency** is a very common cherry in the Midwest, but it's good for all zones. The tree is ten to fifteen feet tall, and the fruit is large, bright red, and roundish in shape. It can be eaten fresh, but since it's tart, it's usually used for all kinds of cooking. Outstanding in pies and the fruit freezes well. Self-pollinating. Zones 3–8.

- **Meteor** has large, light red cherries that mature late in the season. The semidwarf trees get only ten to twelve feet tall and are very hardy in the North, yet they do well in warmer climates, too, and are good in high altitudes. The fruit is large and bright red. Self-pollinating. Zones 2–8.

- **Northstar** has fruit and flesh that is wine-red and somewhat smaller than Montmorency. The tree is a genetic dwarf, growing only six to eight feet tall. The fruit ripens early but hangs on the tree for a couple of weeks. Self-pollinating. Zones 3–8.

Bush Cherries

- **Nanking** cherry, which is a handsome, hardy tree that grows about six to eight feet in height. It has attractive orange-brown branches in winter, which look lovely in the snow. Older bark peels away from the stems in vertical curls that lend interest in the winter landscape. In early spring, pink buds open to white flowers that can withstand a light frost. Nanking cherries are self-pollinating. The fruit is attractive in the early summer and makes the bush glow bright red. Cross-pollination is needed. Zones 2–8.

- **Orient** bush cherry was developed in Minnesota and is self-fertile and produces delicious, medium-large fruit. Zones 3–8.

- **Hansen's** cherry, which gets four to five feet tall. It's self-pollinating and loaded with white flowers in May and sweet purplish-black fruit in July. Good in containers. Zones 3–8.

- **Korean** cherry, or **Flowering Almond,** gets three to five feet tall and is very hardy and very attractive. The tart fruit is firm and the size of sour cherries. The flowers are white to pink. Plant two for good pollination. Zones 2–8.

FRUITING: Sweet cherries bear fruit within three to six years; sour cherries usually bear within three to five years.

YIELD: A standard-sized mature sweet cherry tree can provide up to seventy pounds of fruit per season. Sour cherries yield less, depending on variety, but you should get at least one gallon out of a dwarf tree. Bush cherries produce about fifteen pounds of fruit per bush, depending on variety and growing conditions.

HARVESTING: Cherries become ripe in June and July, depending on variety and growing area.

Sweet cherries and bush cherries need to be picked carefully, with their stems still on the fruit. The technique is to pull gently and twist upward. Sour cherries are not so delicate; sometimes the stem—and even the pit—stays on the tree. The fruit is ready to be picked when it is brightly colored; leave the lighter fruit to ripen.

Neither sweet nor sour cherries ripen after they're harvested.

Cherries in the Kitchen

Sort out any bad cherries and place the fruit in the refrigerator without washing or pitting if you're not using it right away.

PITTING CHERRIES: My mother used to hand pit every cherry using a bobby pin—way too much work! I use my mother-in-law's antique cherry pitter, which is a gadget that you clamp onto the counter and hand-feed the cherries into while turning the crank. The pits come out one place and the cherry flesh comes out another. Much faster and easier than the bobby pin, but not suitable for doing many gallons at one time. It also doesn't hold many cherries in the feeder shoot, so you're constantly hand-feeding it. And you must keep switching low-profile catch pans because the machine wasn't built to work with large bowls. It's better than the pump pitters you sometimes see in catalogues, where you feed each cherry individually and then press a handle to force the pit out.

Instead of pitting the cherries, you can puree them by first simmering the whole cherries and then running them through the fruit and vegetable strainer/food grinder attachment on a KitchenAid mixer. This will separate the pits from the cherry pulp and juice.

Freezing Cherries

DRY PACK: Just place premeasured quantities of the pitted cherries (including the juice) or cherry puree in freezer containers or bags and freeze. I usually use recycled cottage cheese containers, which are just the right size for two or three cups of cherries. Seal, label, and freeze.

SUGAR PACK: I never add sugar before freezing, but some people prefer to mix in 1 part sugar per 4 parts cherries. If you add sugar, be sure to note it on the label so you can later adjust the sugar in recipes.

OTHER: Cooked cherries, as in butters, or baked cherries, as in pies, freeze well.

Eating Cherries

Serving Ideas

- Combine sweet red cherries with sliced pineapple and apricot halves.
- Combine sweet cherries with grapefruit or orange segments and banana slices.

Easy Cherry Ice Cream

1. Place pitted cherries (and any cherry juice that resulted from the pitting) in a food processor and puree to make 2 cups or use cherry sauce.
2. Add the following to the puree and blend in the food processor:

   $1/3$ to $2/3$ cups sugar (reduce, if using sweet cherries)
   1 cup heavy whipping cream or half-and-half or milk
   1 cup sour cream or plain or vanilla yogurt or whipping cream

1 ½ teaspoons vanilla or 2 tablespoons cherry brandy or
 1 tablespoon rum
¼ teaspoon almond extract

3. Pour the mixture into your ice-cream maker and follow the manufacturer's instructions. Stir in toasted almonds slivers, if desired.

Easy Cherry Ice

1. Puree together in a food processor:

3 cups pitted cherries
½ to 1 ¼ cups sugar (reduce if using sweet cherries)
1 ½ cups cranberry juice (or use 1 ¼ cups cranberry juice
 and ¼ cup cherry brandy)

2. Pour the mixture into an ice-cream maker and follow the manufacturer's directions.

Easy Cherry Butter

This recipe is for tart cherries but can be used for sweet cherries if you reduce the sugar.

1. Rinse cherries and pit them.
2. Place cherries in a large saucepan or kettle. Since the pitted cherries will have released some juice, there is no need to add any water. Cook, stirring often, reducing heat once they come to a good simmer.
3. Puree cherries in a food processor or use the cordless blender right in the saucepan.
4. Add sugar to taste, perhaps 3 or 4 cups per gallon of cherries, and cook a few minutes longer until sugar is dissolved.
5. Cool and pour into freezer containers, leaving 1 inch of headspace for expansion. Label, date, and freeze.

NOTE: I once added a carton of cherry butter to cooked, crumbled hamburger, thinking it was my homemade tomato sauce. After I discovered my mistake, I hated the thought of throwing it out. So we sampled the cherry-meat dish and were happy to discover that it tasted great!

Easy Cherry Sauce

1. In a saucepan, combine:

> 3 cups pitted tart cherries
> I cup water
> I tablespoon lemon juice
> ⅔ to I cup sugar

2. Bring the mixture to a boil.
3. Stir 2 tablespoons cornstarch into ½ cup cold water. Add to the sauce and cook together until the liquid thickens and turns clear, 2 or 3 minutes.
4. Remove the sauce from the heat and add 2 tablespoons butter.
5. Chill and serve or freeze.

Old-Fashioned Cherry Pie

1. Combine in a bowl:

> 4 cups pitted tart cherries
> ⅔ to I ½ cups sugar
> ⅓ cup flour
> ⅛ teaspoon salt
> ⅛ teaspoon almond extract (optional)
> 2 tablespoons brandy (optional)
> zest of I lemon (optional)

2. Pour fruit mixture into an unbaked pie shell.
3. Generously dot the filling with pats of butter. Sprinkle generously with cinnamon, if desired.
4. Top with crust and seal the edges. Lightly sprinkle crust with sugar, if desired. Prick crust several times with a paring knife for ventilation.
5. Bake at 425 degrees F for 15 minutes; then reduce the heat to 350 degrees F for about 25–30 minutes or till crust is lightly browned. Serve warm or cold as is, or with a dollop of whipped cream or a scoop of vanilla ice cream.

Easy Cherry Bake

1. In the microwave, melt ½ cup butter in a 2-quart microwave-safe baking pan. Tip pan so butter coats the bottom.

2. Mix together in a bowl, then pour over the melted butter:

> ¾ to 1 cup sugar
> ¾ cup flour
> ¾ cup cream
> 2 teaspoons baking powder

3. Mix together in a bowl, then pour over the batter:

> 2 cups pitted tart cherries
> ¼ to ½ cup sugar
> juice and zest of 1 lemon
> ¼ teaspoon almond extract

4. Bake at 300 degrees F for one hour. The batter will rise to the top as it bakes. Serve as is or top with whipped cream or ice cream.

ELDERBERRIES
IN THE GARDEN

The elderberry is a lovely old-fashioned shrub that is rarely seen, unfortunately. Its flowers are flat-headed clusters of small white blossoms, often six or eight inches across, and they resemble Queen Anne's lace. Each flower develops a small round berry that grows in clusters like the blossoms. The berries have been used to make a dye. The bush is thornless and attractive through all stages of growth. Best of all—you can eat both the blossoms and the fruit!

Why did the beautiful elderberry fall out of favor? Perhaps because people were no longer actively making the traditional jellies, wine, and liqueurs. Or perhaps because the fruit can be messy if the shrub is planted next to a sidewalk or driveway. This problem is avoided by planting the elderberry by itself as a focal point in your yard or perhaps in the center of a bed. Mine is growing in my orchard within view of the house so I can enjoy it all year.

My friend Helen has several wild elderberries that are probably close to the original varieties eaten by the Native Americans. They are lovely, large, rounded bushes, six to eight feet tall, with twiggy branch development rather like a tree.

Elderberry varieties were cultivated long ago from the wild ones used by Native Americans. A large elderberry that had been planted sometime around World War I grew on the east side of the house I lived in as a child. I used the stems and leaves for all sorts of craft projects and the flower heads decorated my mud pies. It was very fruitful, so there may have been two old varieties planted together. Cross-pollination is recommended for the cultivated varieties.

Elderberries are very easy to grow and have more vitamin C than any other garden fruit! They tolerate drought and every climate from zone 2 to 8. You can eat both the blossoms and the berries. Once planted, elderberries require little work and are the most pest-free and disease-free of all berries.

Description

The elderberry is a perennial shrub that blooms in early summer— so there is little worry of frost damage. New hybrids have been developed so that you can choose early, midseason, or late bloomers and thus have a longer supply of the blossoms and the fruit.

The cultivated elderberries produce larger and juicier berries. They usually grow five to ten feet tall, and are upright, although they spread out with age to an eight- or ten-foot diameter for the two bushes needed for best fruiting. There are varieties that grow much taller, however, even to thirty feet. You can control the spread by pruning, if desired.

LOCATION: In your landscaping, where you need a lovely, taller shrub. Some gardeners place a row of them along a fence.

GROWING RANGE: Zones 2 through 8, and temperatures up to 105 degrees F. Do not grow them at altitudes over 8,000 feet.

CHILL REQUIREMENT: None.

SOIL: Elderberries tolerate most soils but prefer a well-drained loam. Mix in well-rotted manure or compost when preparing the planting area.

MOISTURE: They love moisture, but not standing water, and they tolerate drought. If you're going through a drought during fruit development, watering will increase fruit size.

LIGHT: Full sun or partial shade; elderberries like at least half a day of sun.

PLANTING SEASON: Nursery stock can be set out in the spring or the fall, although my recommendation is the spring in northern areas.

HOW TO PLANT:
- Select nursery stock, or plant seeds, or dig up new shoots at the base of established plants in late spring or early summer.
- Till a large hole for the planting so that the roots can be spread out.
- Water weekly until the plant is established.

SUPPORT: None needed.

ONGOING CARE:
- Mulching keeps the elderberries moist and looks nice in the landscaping.
- Weeding will not be necessary because mature shrubs discourage weeds.
- Protecting elderberries from wildlife: Birds like the fruit, although there is so much, you can easily share it. Otherwise, adopt a cat, spread netting, or attach plastic grocery bags as discussed in the section on pests. Birds spread the seeds to other areas, where they can grow as volunteers, but this is easily handled.

PRUNING: Pruning is not needed on the cultivated varieties, but if you have a wild elderberry, you'll probably want to shape the bush occasionally.

POLLINATION: They are self-fruitful, although two varieties planted together increases the yield.

WINTER PROTECTION: Not necessary, except for mulch in very cold areas.

PROPAGATION: Elderberries can be started from seeds or by digging up new shoots at the base in midspring.

VARIETIES INCLUDE:

- **American** elderberry, which is considered the best variety for its fruit quality. Huge ten-inch flower clusters bloom from June to July. The flavorful berries are purplish black. The shrub is fast-growing but short-lived. Zones 3–9.
- **Adams** gets between six and ten feet tall and tolerates moist soil. Ideal for cooking. Plant with Johns for best production. Zones 3–9.
- **Johns** should be planted with Adams for pollination and to produce lots of full-bodied, sweet, medium- or large-sized fruit. Zones 3–9.
- **York** was adapted from Adams to produce the largest of all elderberries. A six- to eight-foot bush with large, creamy white flowers in early summer and vivid fall foliage. Plant with Nova for best pollination. Produces a large crop that ripens after Adams. Zones 4–8.
- **Nova** grows into a six- to eight-foot-tall bush that ripens before York. Produces a heavy crop of large, sweet fruit. Zones 4–8.
- **Variegated** grows light green and white leaves on a shrub six to eight feet tall. Good for cooking. Zones 5–8.

FRUITING: Elderberries produce fruit in their second year.

YIELD: Up to fifteen pounds of berries per mature bush.

HARVESTING: There are two times that you can eat from your elderberry bush: in early summer (usually June–July), when it's in bloom, and late summer (often August–September), when the berries have ripened.

FOR THE BLOSSOMS: Pick the flower heads when the blossoms have fully opened, leaving two or three inches of stem attached.

FOR THE BERRIES: Harvest the berries when they are dark, almost black, in color, by cutting the stem that holds the entire cluster.
 NOTE: The berries don't always mature at the same time. Check daily once they begin to ripen.

Elderberries in the Kitchen

BLOSSOMS: Use the blossoms fresh, or place them in a plastic bag, loosely closed, in the refrigerator. They will keep a few hours, sometimes even a couple of days.

BERRIES: Use the berries right away or refrigerate them in a container lined with paper towels.

Freezing Elderberries

DRY PACK: Clean the berries according to the directions below. Pack the fruit in freezer containers, seal, label and date, and freeze.

OTHER: Elderberry sauce, butter, and pie freeze well.

Eating Elderberry Blossoms

If you haven't done any spraying, use the blossoms without rinsing, or else rinse and place them upside down on a towel to dry before use.

Elderberry Blossoms Browned in Butter

Melt 2 or 3 tablespoons of butter (or olive oil) in a nonstick skillet on medium heat. When the butter is bubbling, place the blossoms in the skillet, heads down, using the stems as a handle. After about 1 minute, or when lightly browned, use the stems to remove the blossoms to a plate lined with paper towels. Serve with the stems attached, and eat the stems and all, or snip them off with kitchen scissors.

Batter-Fried Elderberry Blossoms

Unbelievably good—a rare treat!

Stir together ⅓ cup flour, ¾ teaspoon baking powder, and ¼ teaspoon salt. Gradually add 1 cup cream (can substitute milk but cream is better) to make a smooth batter.

Melt 3 or 4 tablespoons of butter (or olive oil) in a nonstick pan on medium heat. When the butter is bubbly, use the stems to just barely dip the blossoms into the batter and place them in the hot butter, heads down. Remove after 1 or 2 minutes, or when the batter is nicely browned, and place on a plate lined with a paper towel. Add butter as needed to continue. The batter will cover perhaps 2 dozen large flower heads.

Eating Elderberries

Somewhat like blueberries, only smaller, elderberries can be used in a variety of ways. They contain very small seeds that aren't noticeable unless you puree the berries, and even then they aren't a problem to eat. If you don't want the seeds, you can strain the puree.

To use the fresh berries, remove them from their stems. If the fruit isn't too thick in the clusters, you can easily separate the berries with a fork. Hold the cluster by the stem in one hand and rake with the fork in the other hand, starting at the tips of the clusters and working up to the stems, the same way you comb snarls out of long hair.

Once the berries are separated from the stems, pour cold water over them and swish to release any debris. Let the water settle. Most of the unripe berries and any debris will float at the top and most of the ripe berries will settle at the bottom. Carefully pour off the top inch of water and then place the remaining berries in a colander. After they are well drained, the berries are now ready to use or to freeze.

Easy Elderberry Ice Cream

Use sweetened elderberry sauce for this fabulous ice cream. Do not puree the elderberries.

1. Combine:

> 2 cups elderberry sauce (sweetened)
> 2 cups cream or plain yogurt
> ¼ to ½ cup sugar
> 1 ½ teaspoons vanilla or 2 tablespoons dark rum

2. Pour the mixture into your ice-cream maker and follow the manufacturer's instructions.

Easy Elderberry Ice

1. Puree elderberry sauce to make 2 cups. (If desired, you can strain out the tiny seeds, although it's not necessary.)
2. Add about 2 cups crushed pineapple in canned natural juice (either two 8-ounce cans or one 15-ounce can). Puree thoroughly with the elderberries.
3. Pour the mixture into your ice-cream maker and follow the manufacturer's instructions.

Easy Elderberry Sauce or Butter

1. Place elderberries in a large saucepan or kettle that will allow the berries to bubble up without overflowing.
2. For every 1 cup of elderberries, add ½ cup sugar and 4 teaspoons lemon juice.
3. Turn the burner to high heat, stirring constantly for several minutes until the juice is released. Then reduce the heat and simmer for 10 minute for sauce, 20 minutes or longer for butter, stirring occasionally.

4. Remove the elderberries from the heat, cool, and pour into containers. Label, date, and refrigerate or freeze.

NOTE: Unlike many berry recipes, it is not necessary to puree the elderberries for the butter. If you do puree them, the tiny seeds will be released. Although these aren't really a problem to eat, they look unsightly and are hard to strain out because they are so small.

Old-Fashioned Elderberry Pie

1. In a bowl, combine:

> 4 cups elderberries
> ¾ to 1¼ cups sugar
> ½ cup flour
> juice of 1 lemon
> pinch of salt

2. Pour the elderberry mixture into an unbaked pie shell. Dot liberally with butter. Top with crust and seal. Prick crust several times with a paring knife for ventilation.

3. Bake at 400 degrees F for 45 or 50 minutes, or until crust is lightly browned. Serve warm or cold, plain or with ice cream.

GOOSEBERRIES IN THE GARDEN

Gooseberries are a very old fruit that was traditionally grown on farmsteads. The fruit size and shape is anywhere from small and round like marbles to ovals the size of a small chicken egg. The fruit color can be green, white, yellow, red to pink, or purple to black. The gooseberry's unusual name probably came from using the fruit in a sauce served with cooked goose.

Description

Gooseberries grow into an attractive shrub usually between three to five feet tall and wide with arching branches. The leaves are small, one to two inches long and wide, and are lobed rather like maple leaves. The small white flowers bloom early in spring, but they aren't showy.

LOCATION: My gooseberry does well in full sun, but they generally tolerate a little shade, so they can be grown with other bushes in landscaping around the house. Allow four to six feet in diameter per bush.

It's better to plant gooseberries as specimen plants than as a hedge because the branches will lace together, making picking and pruning difficult. Some varieties have thorns, which can be a problem in certain settings.

You can train a gooseberry into a small living topiary tree, by allowing only one branch to grow to form the trunk. See how in "Pruning," below.

NOTE: It has been said that you shouldn't grow gooseberries near cranberries or five-needle pine or you risk disease and insect problems. This ban is supposed to be lifted now, but check on this with your Extension office or local nursery.

GROWING RANGE: Zones 2 through 8. Gooseberries are very hardy and some varieties do well in the far North, although they sometimes get hurt by a late frost.

CHILL REQUIREMENT: Low, but the plants may stay dormant for six months in cold climates.

SOIL: Gooseberries prefer a heavier soil, like loam. They have shallow roots and need ample moisture without standing in water, so need some drainage.

MOISTURE: Gooseberries like average moisture. I must confess I never water my gooseberry, not even in drought years. If you live in a hot climate, you probably will need to water it, especially in the hottest months.

LIGHT: Full sun in the North to light shade in the South.

PLANTING SEASON: Spring or fall.

HOW TO PLANT:
- Till the soil, mixing in well-rotted manure or compost. If the soil is heavy clay, mix in sand for drainage.
- Get good nursery stock rather than planting from a wild variety.
- At planting, prune the tops back to eight or ten inches to encourage bushing.
- Place the plant one inch deeper than it grew at the nursery.
- Tamp the soil after planting, as gooseberries like heavy soil.

- Cover with mulch to keep the weeds down until the plant is established; hoeing could damage the shallow roots.
- If planting in rows, space each plant five feet apart in rows eight feet apart.

SUPPORT: Not needed.

ONGOING CARE:

- Water weekly until the plant is established.
- Mulching is a good idea, although gooseberries will do fine even in mowed grass.
- Fertilize: In the old days, farmers would lay an inch of rotted manure in a three- or four-foot circle around the bush each fall or spring, right on top of mulch, if it was used. If you don't have rotted manure, you can spread one cup of 10-10-10 fertilizer under the bush early in the spring before the buds open. If your soil is poor, you can double the amount. If the leaves look scorched, the plant needs potassium. Spread ½ ounce around the base of the bush each year.

PRUNING: The gooseberry requires little or no work to maintain its shape or control its spread. In very early spring, pruning is done mainly to eliminate old or dead wood and make the bush look tidy.

After the harvest is over, prune out the woody stems over three years old by cutting them off at the ground, because most of the fruit comes on one- and two-year-old stems. You can tell the older branches because they get progressively darker with age.

To increase fruit size, prune the branches back—you'll get less fruit, but it will be larger.

To train a gooseberry into a small tree, allow only one cane to grow from the plant; this will become the trunk. Prune this single trunk back to one and a half to three feet in height, and it will start branch growth at the cut. Then prune these branches back to six inches to stimulate a nice dense ball. Keep removing any branches or leaves that form lower on the trunk. This will look like an ornamental "mop head" tree you would pay a fortune to buy, but unlike the nursery ornamentals, these will bear fruit.

NOTE: If the tree trunk should winter-kill, you probably have lost the whole tree, whereas if a branch in the shrub form dies, the bush still has others.

POLLINATION: Gooseberries are self-pollinating.

WINTER PROTECTION: Two inches of mulch is helpful, but not essential. If you have a problem with mice, keep the mulch pulled back two inches from the canes.

PROPAGATION: Layering or stem cuttings.

VARIETIES INCLUDE:
- **Pixwell,** which has few thorns and large light-green berries that ripen to pale pink with pink flesh. When ripe, the gooseberries are juicy, sweet, and soft. Good for cooking. A drought-tolerant variety. Leaves turn purple in the fall. Zones 3–9.
- **Poorman** is a larger bush with few thorns that grows quickly. The large, one-inch fruit is green, turning to wine-red when ripe and has an excellent flavor when eaten raw or cooked. Considered to be our best gooseberry. Zones 4–10.
- **Welcome** is a nearly thornless, willowy bush that produces medium-sized light-green fruit that ripens to rosy-red in midsummer. Bears from mid-June to late July. Better flavored than Pixwell. Especially suited for the mid-Atlantic states. Zones 4–7.
- **Oregon Champion** grows three to five feet tall and produces medium to large, pale yellowish-green berries. Excellent for cooking. Suited for the Northwest. Zones 4–10.
- **Hinnomaki Red** is from Finland. The bush is about four feet tall and three feet wide and produces medium red fruit that is good either fresh or cooked. Ripens midsummer. Zones 4–7.
- **Hinnomaki Yellow** is also from Finland. It has small yellowish-green fruit that tastes a bit like apricots. Ripens midsummer. Extremely hardy. Zones 2–9.

FRUITING: Sometimes you'll get a crop starting in the second year after planting, but usually it's the third or fourth year. The plant won't be fully productive for five to ten years.

YIELD: Usually four to six quarts, sometimes up to ten quarts, per plant.

HARVESTING: Harvest time can be late spring through summer, depending on variety. The fruit is ripe when it falls easily into your hand. The gooseberries don't all ripen at once, so the harvest might continue over two or three weeks.

Be careful to shade your bucket as you pick the gooseberries, because they can burn in the sun.

NOTE: People who don't like gooseberries might have eaten the fruit before it's ripe.

Gooseberries in the Kitchen

Gooseberries are an old farm staple. They can be eaten fresh out of the garden, but farmwives used them more often in pies. Gooseberries keep well for a few days in the refrigerator.

The flavor varies greatly with the variety grown, and also varies from year to year due to different conditions, much like grapes.

Freezing Gooseberries

Remove stems, wash in cold water, and drain the gooseberries.

DRY PACK: Lay the fruit in a single layer and freeze. When frozen, pack the fruit in freezer bags or containers and return to the freezer. Or pack the gooseberries directly into freezer bags or containers. Seal, label, and freeze.

SUGAR PACK: Some people like to add sugar to the gooseberries before freezing them, at the ratio of ⅔ cup sugar per quart of gooseberries. Be sure to note the added sugar on the label so that you can later adjust recipes, if necessary.

OTHER: Gooseberry butter, sauce, and pie freeze well.

Eating Gooseberries

To eat, just rinse and use them as is, although some people remove the stem and the bottom with kitchen shears.

Stewed gooseberries can be folded into whipped cream, which is a very old serving method from Europe.

Easy Gooseberry Ice Cream

1. Using drained gooseberry sauce, puree the gooseberries to make 2 cups.
2. Add 1 cup pineapple with its juice, 1 cup sugar, and 1½ cups cream. Puree together.
3. Pour the mixture into your ice-cream maker and follow the manufacturer's instructions.

NOTE: Gooseberries have small seeds. If these are objectionable, strain them out of the gooseberry puree before adding the other ingredients.

Easy Gooseberry Ice

1. Using drained gooseberry sauce, puree the gooseberries to make 3 cups.
2. Add 1½ cups pineapple with its own juice and 1⅓ cups sugar. Puree well.
3. Pour the mixture into your ice-cream maker and follow the manufacturer's instructions.

NOTE: Gooseberries have small seeds. If these are objectionable, strain them out of the gooseberry puree before adding the other ingredients.

Gooseberry Butter

Crush gooseberries with a potato masher and place them in a saucepan or kettle if doing a larger batch. Add a little water and bring the gooseberries to a simmer, stirring constantly. Add 1½ to 2 cups of sugar for every 3 cups of gooseberries, and orange or lemon zest to taste, if desired. Simmer a few minutes longer until fruit is tender or until thickened. Pour into containers. Store in the refrigerator or freeze.

Gooseberry Sauce

Cook gooseberries in a saucepan or kettle in the following proportions: for every 2 cups of gooseberries, add 1 cup water and ½ to 1 cup sugar. Simmer until the gooseberries are tender. Refrigerate or freeze in the cooking liquid. Serve with a dollop of whipped cream or vanilla ice cream.

Old-Fashioned Gooseberry Pie

1. In a saucepan, combine:

> 1 cup gooseberries, crushed
> 1 1/4 to 1 1/2 cups sugar
> 1/3 cup flour
> pinch salt
> 1/4 teaspoon almond extract

2. Then add 2 cups whole gooseberries.
3. Cook over medium heat, stirring constantly, until mixture thickens somewhat.
4. Pour mixture into an unbaked pie shell. Dot liberally with butter and top with crust. Prick crust several times with a paring knife for ventilation. Sprinkle top crust lightly with sugar, if desired.
5. Bake at 400 degrees F for 45 minutes or until crust is lightly browned. Serve warm or cold, with whipped cream or vanilla ice cream, if desired.
   NOTE: Immature, hard gooseberries make the best pies.

GRAPES IN THE GARDEN

Grapes were allowed to grow wild in the grove of many farmsteads of old, climbing up trees or shrubs, growing on fences around fields, or trailing alongside raspberries in a delightful tangle. This is a no-work method for those who have the space, but harvest can be a challenge and the size and flavor of many grapes is reduced unless the vines are pruned.

You can get stock for grapes with or without seeds, and the fruit can be green, pink, purple, red, or white. Table grapes are sweeter than those raised especially for wine. The harvest can be early, mid-, or late season. There are many, many choices for you, depending on what kinds of grapes you prefer and what you want to do with them. Be sure to select vines appropriate for your growing conditions.

Before you decide to grow grapes, you need to consider two important things: the site and the support.

Description

Grapes grow on perennial vines that are attractive enough to incorporate into the landscape.

LOCATION: When choosing a spot for grapes, think first about your wind conditions, and try to select a location where they will be protected from severe wind and yet still get good air circulation.

Next, consider slope. Grapes like to grow on a slope to help prevent frost from settling in the spring or fall, and also to keep the air moving, to help prevent fungal disease. The ideal slope is to the east or southeast, but a south or southwest slope is almost as good.

Since grapes are a vining plant, they will fit into any landscaping plan. Grow them on a trellis against the house, on an arbor shading your deck, as a privacy screen along the property line, or along your deck railing. I've even grown grapes in containers.

GROWING RANGE: Although many grapes will grow only in warm climates, there are varieties for zones 4 through 8, and even a few that go into zones 2 or 3.

CHILL REQUIREMENT: Depending on variety, between 100 and 500 hours below 45 degrees F.

SOIL: Grapes thrive even in poor or rocky soil so long as it is well drained and deep. Grapes like gravelly loam, but will do well even in clay or heavy soils if you add sand for good drainage. If the soil is too rich, the vines will grow profusely but the fruit will come in less quantity and inferior quality.

Rotted manure is the best fertilizer, or use one half-cup of 10-10-10 fertilizer at the base of each vine in early spring.

MOISTURE: The first year, grapes need one inch of water each week, so you'll need to hand water if there isn't enough rain. Don't spray the vines, or water with a mist, because this could promote disease. You need to direct the moisture at the roots, where it is needed. After the vines are established, they seldom need watering and they can withstand drought and heat. If grapes are overwatered, their leaves will drop.

LIGHT: Grapes need sun but can grow in partial shade, although this will reduce the yield.

PLANTING SEASON: Late spring.

HOW TO PLANT:

- Before beginning, have the grapes' support in place.
- Use one-year-old nursery stock.
- Till the soil deeply and add well-rotted manure or compost, and sand, if needed for drainage.
- Dig the hole deep and wide enough to spread out the grapes' roots without cramping them.
- Be careful not to plant the vine deeper than it was from the nursery, because that would encourage suckers from the rootstock below the graft.
- Insert a stake in the hole without damaging the roots, to support the vine if there is no other support nearby.
- Tamp the ground so the roots are firmly anchored.
- Space the vines six to eight feet apart, or as recommended by the nursery.
- Mulch to keep moisture in and weeds out for the first year.
- Water well at planting and maintain a watering schedule the first summer, to get the plants established.
- Start training the vines; see "Pruning," below.

SUPPORT: Grapes must have some kind of support, and it needs to be in place before you plant the vines: Because grape roots are shallow, they spread out several feet and are easily damaged. Give it a lot of thought.

If you prefer wood, choose cedar, redwood, or teak that won't rot and will not require future painting or staining, as you won't have access to do it. Beware of the chemicals that are used in pressure-treated lumber as these can be harmful. We're great fans of the new vinyl-covered railings and fencings that never need paint and won't discolor or crack in the sun or cold. Any of these can be used as posts in the ground to support the vines planted below and then allowed to grow horizontally on wire strung between the posts.

There are lots of structures you can buy or make that would provide wonderful support and even be quite decorative in your landscape. Short on money? I know people who trained their grapes up old clothesline supports and the vines followed the wires from the post. Another person put strong wire fencing along the side of her house and trained the vines on it in tiers like espalier.

When The Farmer helped me start my grapes, we buried ten-foot-long posts three feet in the ground, using a posthole digger powered by his tractor—this depth was more than most will need; we have very strong winds. You most likely could get by with four-inch diameter posts buried two feet in the ground. Just be sure that the posts can bear the weight of the vines and the fruit as well as resist the tension of the wires.

We set six posts in two rows, six feet apart each way. When putting the soil back into the hole, be sure to tamp it down—use a stick or rod or tamping tool.

Next, we strung wire between the posts at six and a half feet and again halfway to the ground so that we'd have two tiers. I used strong 11- or 12-gauge galvanized farm wire, but some people think using copper wire discourages diseases, because copper has antifungal properties.

We planted grapes at the base of each corner post, and two on each side of the two center posts; eight plants in all.

We trained the vine to one stem, or leader, that grew to the first cross-wire. There, buds grew along the wires, as we trained the leader up to the top wire and allowed buds to grow horizontally along this tier. The vines were tied with old pantyhose cut in strips.

It looked great and the grapes grew well. But the story doesn't have a happy ending. A few years later, I lost seven of the eight grape varieties when the county weed commissioner was spraying ditches and the wind carried the chemical to my grapes. I was outside at the time, some distance from the spray, and even my clothes and hair smelled of the chemical. Beware of using any lawn or garden chemicals— grapes are very sensitive to chemical weed controls and the slightest whiff will kill them.

ONGOING CARE: Mulching is not necessary once the vines are established, because the roots can go very deep and they actually prefer to be slightly dry.

If birds are a problem, cover the vines with netting just before the grapes ripen—with my cat population, I've never had to do this. Some gardeners staple small paper sacks over the grapes.

If insects are a problem, spray the vines with a pyrethrum spray or other insecticide (see the "Sources" section). Or try to encourage some "pet" snakes!

If disease is a problem, do what you can to promote air circulation and use a Bordeaux spray.

Check with your local Extension for information about grape problems in your area and spraying recommendations. It is possible to grow grapes and never have to spray, by choosing the correct varieties, siting and supporting them properly, etc.

NOTE: Grapes can send roots out in a fifteen-foot radius, so beware of using lawn chemicals, as these can be picked up by the roots, perhaps killing the grapes.

PRUNING: Some people maintain rigid control over their grapes' growth by pruning. But I've also seen vines succeed when they have been allowed to grow pretty much as they wished, except for thinning for aeration. If you don't want to prune grapes, don't—they will grow perfectly well if left on their own. You can train them to a trellis or arbor and let them go. One friend had vines along a wall that fanned out in all directions, pruning only when the vines got out of bounds, and they still produced well. Even with little or no pruning, you will still have plenty to harvest and eat, and probably even enough to give away.

So, why prune, aside from keeping the vines neat and tidy? The main purpose of pruning grapes is to encourage fruiting, because the fruit comes on the one-year-old wood, and you'll keep new shoots in development. Also, pruning keeps the vines from becoming too dense, reducing air circulation, which might cause problems with disease.

Professional vintners use a strict pruning approach, but the following would work for a home gardener growing American grape varieties:

- Right after planting, prune each grape so that only the best cane remains, becoming the "leader." This will be the main trunk of the vine, and it will thicken with age.
- Tie this trunk onto the support and keep removing any side shoots until the vine reaches the desired height—this usually takes two or three years.
- Prune the trunk at the desired height. This will stimulate side branches to grow. Select the best three and train one to go to the right, and the other to the left. Allow the third one to continue growing up to the next level, then prune it and train two more side branches.
- When the leader is as tall as you want it to get, cut it off diagonally through a bud—this will stop further growth.
- If you have an arbor, pergola, or other such structure, you can allow the vine's top shoots to fan out over the top for a lovely effect. If you've attached wire mesh to a wall, you can allow the grape vines to fan out. Or train only two side shoots to grow horizontally along the top of a fence, deck railing, or, in my case, on the lowest wire. My vines then continued growing to the top wire, and the process was repeated.

In cold climates, pruning is best done in the spring, although pruning to remove unwanted growth can be done anytime except when the vines freeze, because then they are brittle and easily damaged.

Keep this in mind: Some grapes produce larger clusters than others. The larger the size of these clusters, the more the fruiting vines should be shortened by pruning, or else you need to remove some of the clusters. For example, Concord vines can support perhaps fifty grape clusters without problems, but Thompson Seedless grapes can ripen only perhaps ten clusters. If the vines aren't pruned or the fruit clusters thinned, the grapes could have poor color and taste due to low sugar, or the grapes could stress and damage the vines.

NOTE: Save the healthy pruned vines. They can be used for all sorts of craft projects, including wreath making.

POLLINATION: Most grapes are self-pollinating, so you can get by with one plant of each type you want.

WINTER PROTECTION: Increase the mulch thickness. If the vines are at risk, some gardeners remove them from their supports, lay them on the ground, and cover them with one foot of leaves.

PROPAGATION: Stem, leaf, or root cuttings. I've never failed to have a vine root when I bend it to the ground and put a little soil or mulch over the end. You might have to attach it to the ground with an earth staple, which you can make from a length of wire bent in half. After the vine tip is well rooted, cut the connection to the parent plant, dig the new plant, and transplant it where desired. I've also been successful at growing grapes from seeds.

VARIETIES INCLUDE:
- **Concord**, an old grape that's easy to grow and very hardy. It has round purple fruit that have a lot of juice and a tart taste. It ripens in late September, and the vines are very productive. The problem with the old Concord variety was the seeds, which should be removed for the best eating. Now there is a seedless Concord variety, which has smaller fruit clusters, but there are thirty or forty clusters per vine. The seedless Concord grows in zones 5–9 and in some parts of zone 4.

- **Seedless Pink Reliance** has pretty pink grapes that are big and plump and great for eating. The fruit ripens in late August and yields forty to fifty clusters per vine. Zones 4–8
- **Seedless Thompson** has pale green fruit that is sweet and delicious eaten fresh. Each vine yields twenty to thirty clusters. Zones 4–8.
- **Seedless Red Canadice** is the hardiest of red grapes. The fruit has tender skin and is great for eating in late August through early September. Zones 4–8.

FRUITING: Grapes usually take about three years to bear fruit.

YIELD: Eight pounds or more per vine, depending on variety.

HARVESTING: Harvest the fruit by snapping off or cutting off the entire cluster, leaving about one inch of stem attached to the cluster.

Be sure to check the grapes often as they get close to their harvest time. A good test is to try one—if it tastes sweet, the grapes are ready. Also check the color of the seeds, if your variety has seeds: The seeds will turn from green to brown when the fruit is ripe. Ripe grapes can be removed from the vine fairly easily.

Be careful not to pile the harvested fruit too deep, because the weight will crush the lower grapes.

Be careful, also, of snakes. Fortunately, we have only the non-poisonous variety in our area. The Farmer calls them my pets because I allow snakes to live in my yard and gardens—they are useful as they eat lots of troublesome insects. One fall, The Farmer was helping me with the grape harvest, directing me to a large cluster I could reach but not see. He didn't realize one of my "pets" was hanging in the vines nearby. Instead of touching a bunch of juicy grapes, my fingers closed around the belly of a warm snake! You can imagine how quickly I recoiled—and The Farmer laughed and laughed! Finally, he said, "I thought you weren't afraid of snakes!" I'm not, but that doesn't mean I want to handle them!

Grapes in the Kitchen

Store harvested grapes in the refrigerator in perforated plastic bags—these can be purchased or you can punch holes in a regular plastic bag. Grapes will keep about two weeks.

Freezing Grapes

I do not like the rubbery texture of frozen grapes, so recommend that you do not freeze the grapes whole, although it can be done using the dry pack method.

OTHER: Grapes are best frozen as a puree, butter, or juice. Package in freezer containers, seal, label, and freeze.

Eating Grapes

Grapes can be eaten raw, added to salads, or topped with whipped cream or vanilla pudding.

To remove the seeds, first cook the grapes, then strain them through a fine sieve or double layer of cheesecloth.

Serving Ideas

- Combine grapes, orange or grapefruit segments, and banana slices.
- Combine grapes, watermelon and cantaloupe balls, and shredded coconut.
- Combine grapes with diced pineapple.

Grape Ice Cream

1. Combine the following:

> 2 cups grape puree (to make puree without seeds, cook
> the grapes briefly in very little water and then run
> them through a food mill or use the fruit and veg-
> etable strainer/food grinder attachment on a
> KitchenAid mixer or coarsely puree grapes in the
> food processor, then strain out the seeds and skins)
> I cup heavy cream
> I cup sour cream (NOTE: You can substitute plain
> yogurt for the cream and sour cream if desired.)
> 1/3 to 2/3 cup sugar
> 1/2 teaspoon vanilla

2. Pour the mixture into your ice-cream maker and follow the manufacturer's instructions.
   NOTE: This mixture is not as thick as my other ice cream mixtures,
but do not worry, it still freezes up in a short time to a nice texture.

Easy Grape Ice

1. Combine the following:

> 2 cups grape juice or puree (see Grape Ice Cream
> recipe, above, for instructions)
> 1/3 cup sugar
> 1 1/2 cups pineapple juice
> I cup orange juice

2. Pour the mixture into your ice-cream maker and follow the manufacturer's instructions.

Easy Grape Butter

This recipe works with any kind of grapes.

1. Put grapes in a large saucepan or kettle with a little water, perhaps
   1/4 cup per gallon of grapes. Cook on medium heat, stirring and
   mashing the grapes. When the grapes have thickened, run them
   through a food mill to remove the seeds and skins. If your grapes are

seedless, there is no need to run them through the food mill; instead, puree the grapes with their skins for added flavor and nutrients.

2. Return the grape puree to the stove and cook another 15 or 20 minutes. Add sugar, perhaps 1 to 2 cups per gallon of grapes, although this is optional, depending on the tartness of your grapes. As an alternative sweetener, stir in a little honey after the puree has thickened and has started to cool, but this is also optional.

3. Cool and pour into freezer containers, leaving 1 inch of headspace for expansion. Seal, label, date, and freeze.

Mom's Grape Juice

1. Cook grapes in a little water, perhaps ¼ cup per gallon of grapes, until tender.

2. Run the grapes through a food mill to separate out the skins and seeds.

3. Let the juice stand and then pour off the sediment that rises to the top. Pour or ladle the juice without disturbing the sediment on the bottom, which should be discarded.

4. Add ½ cup sugar per quart (this is for our tart grapes—you might need less or none). Stir until sugar is dissolved.

5. Chill and serve. Or pour into freezer containers, allowing headspace. Seal, label and date, and freeze.

Grape Pudding

Surprisingly good!

1. In a saucepan, combine:

> 1 cup sugar
> ½ cup quick tapioca
> ½ teaspoon salt

2. Stir in:

> 4 cups grape juice
> 2 tablespoons lemon juice

3. Cook over low heat just until mixture comes to a boil, stirring constantly. Remove from heat. Chill and serve.

Easy Grape Pie

We love this!

1. In an unbaked pie shell, place 3 or 4 cups of seedless grapes.
2. Combine the following and pour over the grapes:

> ¾ cup sugar
> ¼ cup quick tapioca
> 1 cup heavy cream, gradually stirred into the sugar and
>   tapioca

3. Dot the filling with butter and sprinkle with cinnamon, if desired.
4. Top with crust and seal the edges. Lightly sprinkle crust with sugar, if desired. Prick crust several times with a paring knife for ventilation.
5. Bake at 425 degrees F for 40 to 45 minutes or until the crust is lightly browned. Serve warm or cold as is, or with a dollop of whipped cream or scoop of vanilla ice cream.

KIWIS IN THE GARDEN

Hardy kiwis are beautiful vines with shiny green foliage. They grow well in cold winters without protection through zone 3, they tolerate either shade or sun, and they rarely have problems with diseases or pests, not even birds. Unlike the fuzzy fruit you buy in the grocery store, the hardy kiwis have smooth skins that don't require peeling.

The only problem with hardy kiwis is that the vines have either male or female flowers and you usually must get both if you want fruit. You can't tell one from the other when you're buying them, so you must trust that the nursery has done a good job of identifying the sex and that the labels haven't been accidentally switched. I ordered a pair some years ago that were supposed to be male and female, yet they never set fruit, so obviously someone made a mistake.

Description

A perennial vine, often either male or female, with the females producing smooth-skinned fruits. The more cold-tolerant the vine, the smaller the fruit. The kiwis are extremely high in vitamin C.

LOCATION: Kiwis are beautiful in the landscape but must get sturdy support (see "Support," below). Also, remember that many varieties need to have both a male and a female for pollination. A north-facing slope is ideal for kiwi. If the kiwi can be positioned so it is shielded from low winter sun and early spring sun, it will survive harsh winters better.

GROWING RANGE: Hardy kiwis can be grown in nearly the entire United States and parts of Canada. (Chinese kiwi, the fuzzy kind in the store, is hardy only to 10 degrees F, and need a longer growing season than it can get in most of the United States.)

CHILL REQUIREMENT: Between 800 and 900 hours, depending on the variety.

SOIL: Hardy kiwis like light soil but tolerate many soils, so long as the soil has drainage.

MOISTURE: Kiwis have shallow roots that like moisture so long as they're not in soggy soil or standing water.

LIGHT: Full sun to part shade, with some varieties very shade tolerant. In hot climates, kiwis do best in partial shade.

PLANTING SEASON: Spring.

HOW TO PLANT:
- Select nursery stock appropriate for your area.
- Till the soil well, adding well-rotted manure or compost, and sand, if needed.
- Plant the vines at the same depth they grew at the nursery, and allow the roots to spread out.

SUPPORT: Kiwis need sturdy support, which should be in place before planting the vines. We used old decorative wrought-iron posts and panels anchored in the ground in our orchard, which was quite attractive. Some people use old clotheslines and poles for their kiwis with success. Kiwis can be trained to grow on top of fences. They climb up the sides of buildings and are lovely on gazebos and pergolas. Whatever your choice, kiwis need to be tied to the support.

ONGOING CARE: Provide winter protection the first two or three years.

Some gardeners say you should protect the vines from cats because kiwis have the same attraction to cats as catnip, but I never had that problem, even with an outdoor herd of twenty felines!

PRUNING: Summer pruning consists in keeping the vines neat, removing shoots from the trunk, and controlling the overall shape as desired.

Just like grapes or espalier, cutting the trunk stimulates the buds to grow, and these can be trained into the permanent branches that grow into the pattern you desire. Once you've established the shape and size you want, pruning is just a matter of maintenance. You can do nothing and the vines will produce fruit, but kiwi is vigorous and you'll probably want to prune it to keep it in bounds.

Since male plants do not produce fruit, they have a lot of energy to put into vine growth. Unless you want them for ornamental purposes, male plants can be pruned severely after blooming, since they are needed only for pollen. To do this, cut each flowering shoot back to where it's developing a new shoot, removing about three-quarters of the entire vine. This will stimulate the development of new flower buds for the next year.

POLLINATION: As many as eight female vines can be pollinated by one male if the male is located within thirty-five to one hundred feet. Closer is better, especially if you don't have many bees, because they must carry the pollen to the female flowers.

WINTER PROTECTION: Since winters sometimes have occasional warming spells, you can lay corn stalks or canna tops over the vines and tie them to the support. This will prevent them from wasting their energy by prematurely budding, and is necessary only the first couple of years unless you live in areas with wildly fluctuating temperatures. For best results, apply the winter protection after the frost is in the ground.

PROPAGATION: Propagation is by cuttings, grafting, and seeds.

You can mash the fresh fruit with a fork and plant the seeds, pulp and all. Mark the spot because you won't see growth until the next spring. The seeds need at least two months of cool weather before they will germinate.

VARIETIES INCLUDE:

- **Hardy Subzero** kiwi will withstand the coldest winters, even in zone 3, and has bright green kiwis that are sweeter than the fuzzy type sold in stores. You need to have both a male and a female plant.
- **Hardy Red** kiwis have red fruit with a sweet-tart flavor, which ripen mid- to late fall. Requires a pollinator. Zones 4–9
- **Issai** kiwi is the vine usually chosen if you want fruit—and best of all, it doesn't require a pollinator, although fruiting is increased if you have a male; without a male, the fruit is seedless. The leaves are entirely green and the flowers are white. It usually fruits in the second year but sometimes will bear the first year it's planted. Fruit size is anywhere between that of grapes and plums, and it ripens late summer/early fall. It tastes like the fuzzy kiwi from the store. Zones 5–9.
- **Artic Beauty** leaves are green tinged with bright pink and white. The male is the most colorful and is often grown as an ornamental. The female bears fruit early, even in the first year. The fruit is rather small, about three quarters of an inch in diameter, but sweet and delicious; harvest in early fall. Very shade-tolerant. Very hardy, survives to zone 2.

FRUITING: Kiwis often produce fruit in the second year, usually in late summer or early fall.

YIELD: A mature, well-managed hardy kiwi vine can produce twenty to one hundred pounds of fruit in a season.

HARVESTING: The one- to one-and-a-half-inch fruit is not completely ripe when it's harvested in late summer. To test, pick several fruits and allow them to sit on the counter a few days; then taste them. If they are sweet, they're ready for harvest.

Kiwis in the Kitchen

Unlike the fuzzy store-bought kiwis, which are usually peeled, hardy kiwis are eaten skin and all. Kiwis keep in the refrigerator for a long time, even several months, if placed in a plastic bag with a few breathing holes punched in it and kept cold and humid. You still must allow them to soften on the counter or ripen in a paper sack with an apple.

Freezing Kiwi

DRY PACK: Kiwi can be frozen whole, although some people feel they turn astringent unless they are cut into ¼-inch slices. If the kiwis are tart, sprinkle the slices with a little sugar. Pack in freezer containers or bags, label and freeze.

OTHER: Kiwi butter or sauce can be frozen.

Eating Kiwi

Kiwis make great fruit ices and are wonderful additions when added to salads. Cooking should not be done with high heat, as the kiwis turn tart and brownish green.

Easy Kiwi Ice Cream

1. Puree fresh kiwi in a food processor to make 1 cup.
2. Add the following to the puree and blend in the food processor:
   > ½ cup pineapple juice
   > ½ to ¾ cup sugar
   > 1 ½ cups heavy whipping cream
   > ½ cup half-and-half (NOTE: you can substitute plain
   >   vanilla yogurt for the cream and half-and-half, if
   >   desired)
   > ½ teaspoon vanilla
3. Pour the mixture into your ice-cream maker and follow the manufacturer's instructions.

Kiwi Ice

1. Puree fresh kiwi in a food processor to make 3 cups. (Note: You can substitute strawberries or pineapple for part of the kiwi.)
2. Add:

   1/3 to 2/3 cup sugar
   1 1/2 cups pineapple juice

3. Pour the mixture into your ice-cream maker and follow the manufacturer's instructions. If you don't have an ice-cream maker, put the mixture in your regular freezer in a wide metal bowl and remove it after 15 minutes and beat it well. Repeat this several times until firm enough to serve.

Kiwi Sauce

1. Cut kiwi into slices about 3/8-inch thick. Measure the kiwi and then place it in a saucepan. (NOTE: You can substitute sliced strawberries for part of the kiwi.)
2. Per 1 cup of fruit, add between 1 and 3 tablespoons sugar and 1/4 cup pineapple juice.
3. Stirring constantly, bring the mixture to a boil, then reduce heat and simmer 1 minute for sauce, until kiwi is just cooked.
4. Remove from heat and serve warm. Or cool and place in containers. Label and refrigerate or freeze.

Kiwi Butter

1. Pulse kiwi in the food processor so that it is very coarsely chopped. Measure the kiwi and then place it in a saucepan. (NOTE: You can substitute strawberries for part of the kiwi.)
2. Per 1 cup of kiwi, add between 1 and 3 tablespoons sugar and 1/4 cup pineapple juice.
3. Stirring constantly, bring mixture to a boil, then reduce heat and simmer, stirring occasionally, until it is somewhat thickened. Puree in the pan with the hand blender or use a food processor, and if it isn't thick enough for butter, simmer it a little longer.

4. Remove from heat, cool, and place in containers. Label and refrigerate or freeze.

Easy Kiwi Pie

1. Combine in a bowl:

> 3 cups sliced kiwi
> 1 cup crushed pineapple, drained
> 1/2 to 3/4 cup sugar
> 3 to 4 tablespoons quick tapioca (amount depends on
>   how juicy the kiwis are)

2. Pour fruit mixture into an unbaked pie shell.
3. Generously dot the filling with pats of butter.
4. Top with crust and seal edges. Lightly sprinkle crust with sugar, if desired. Prick crust several times with a paring knife for ventilation.
5. Bake at 350 degrees F about 35 to 40 minutes or till crust is lightly browned and the kiwi are tender when a paring knife is inserted into the crust. Serve warm or cold as is, in a bowl topped with cream, or with a dollop of whipped cream or a scoop of vanilla ice cream.

Sour Cream Kiwi Dessert

This recipe uses six individual dessert dishes that are ovenproof and hold 1 to 1 1/2 cups of liquid each. Custard cups are too small for these servings.

1. Place about 1/2 cup sliced kiwi in the bottom of each dessert dish. Sprinkle a teaspoon of white sugar over the fruit. Top with a little lemon zest (optional, but tasty!).
2. Mix together:

> 1/2 cup sugar
> 1/2 cup brown sugar, packed
> 1/4 cup flour
> 1 cup sour cream

3. Pour a scant 1/3 cup of batter over each dish of kiwi slices.
4. Bake for 30 minutes at 350 degrees F. Serve warm or cold.

MULBERRIES
IN THE GARDEN

In days of old, many farmsteads had a few mulberry trees growing back in their groves, usually in a sunny spot away from the house. They were also planted to provide shade for chicken yards and hog lots, and the fruit that fell was quickly gobbled up, providing rich nutrition. The quick-growing trees were a source of wood for fence posts on long-ago farms.

We had several trees growing alongside a field, and the fruit made wonderful pies. Unfortunately, a neighbor one mile south had problems with his combine at harvest time. His machine threw out sparks, igniting a field fire that traveled for over three miles before it could be contained, destroying all my mulberry trees as well as our crops. All the neighboring farmers quit harvesting their fields and ran to get their tractors and disks to plow under our fields ahead of the fire, in hopes of containing it. It is heartbreaking to destroy crops, but it had to be done or every one of us might have lost not only our harvest, but also our homes and all our expensive farm machinery as well. The corn and soybean plants were dry and ignited easily into a raging inferno. Firemen came from several nearby communities to help battle the flames, which reached two hundred feet in the air and were whipped into a frenzy by a strong wind. Field fires are not only costly, but extremely dangerous. Now I get my mulberries from a neighbor, whose trees, fortunately, were spared.

Mulberry trees are wonderfully tolerant of drought, they'll adapt to almost any soil so long as they're not in standing water, and they can even withstand city pollution. Although our trees were very old, we didn't have any disease or pest problems. Birds love the berries, which is not a problem because the berries are so abundant that there are plenty to share.

Although mulberries are quick growing, it takes about ten years before they produce fruit. The mulberry is extremely hardy, growing even in cold northern areas, which makes them a good substitute in climates unfriendly to blackberries. Unlike other fruiting trees that are lovely in the spring, the blossoms on mulberries are inconspicuous. The trees can live up to three hundred years, bearing fruit their whole lives!

Description

The mulberry is a good shade tree, growing twenty-five to forty or sometimes even sixty feet tall, but it is grown more for its fruit. Mulberries resemble blackberries, although they are somewhat smaller and have a slightly different flavor. My trees had some leaves with one lobe, resembling mittens; some with two lobes, one on each side; and some with no lobes—all together in clusters. I get fruit from a neighbor who has trees like mine as well as one mulberry tree with glossy, unlobed leaves—and I've found the fruit from the latter to be slightly superior.

LOCATION: Since the fruit is messy, don't plant mulberries near a patio, sidewalk, or parking area.

GROWING RANGE: Mulberries can be grown in zones 2 through 8. They are slow to bud in the spring, so the blooms and fruit are saved from frost damage.

CHILL REQUIREMENT: A minimum of four hundred hours under 45 degrees F, depending on the variety.

SOIL: Almost any soil, so long as the roots are not in standing water.

MOISTURE: Water to get the tree established, but then it is tolerant of drought.

LIGHT: Although the tree will tolerate some shade, when grown in a grove, plant it in full sun for the most flavorful berries.

PLANTING SEASON: Spring.

HOW TO PLANT: Refer to tree planting instructions in the "Garden Notes" section. Space mulberry trees thirty feet apart.

SUPPORT: None.

ONGOING CARE: None, after watering the first year or two.

PRUNING: Only if necessary to remove dead or damaged branches.

POLLINATION: Mulberries are considered to be self-pollinating, although two trees increase the yield. However, they can pollinate over a long distance, which might be why they are thought to self-pollinate. Young trees can produce all male flowers one year, all female flowers another year, and both male and female in still another year.

WINTER PROTECTION: None.

PROPAGATION: Mulberries are propagated from seeds and green-wood cuttings, and are sometimes grafted.

VARIETIES INCLUDE:
- **New American,** which is said to have the best fruit. The fruits are like blackberries and are good fresh or cooked. Zones 4–8.
- **Northrop** is extremely hardy and grows very rapidly. Zones 2–8.
- **Oscar**'s fruit tastes like raspberries and is edible when in

the red stage but is black when fully ripened. Tolerates bad conditions, including drought. Zones 5–9.

- **Black Beauty** is a semidwarf mulberry that grows to fifteen feet tall. To Zone 4.
- **Paradise** is a dwarf mulberry that gets about seven feet tall and produces sweet whitish berries. Zones 5–8.

FRUITING: It takes about ten years for the first crop. Like cane berries, mulberries flower and produce fruit on new growth, on the ends of the shoots.

YIELD: Many gallons of fruit per mature tree.

HARVESTING: Mulberries ripen from early summer to midsummer; in my area this means late June into July. The fruit doesn't mature all at once, so you will see greenish white berries, red berries, and dark purple-black berries together in clusters. Pick only the purple ones, which fall off the branch when they are barely touched.

You can hold a container and handpick the ripe mulberries, or you can do it our easy way. Spread a clean cloth under the tree—it could be an old bedspread, old sheet, etc.—and gently shake the tree branches. Only the dark berries will fall off, and these are the ripe ones.

Ripe mulberries are fragile, so do not pile them deep in a bucket as the weight of the fruit will crush the lower berries.

NOTE: Mulberries can stain clothing, so be sure to wear old clothes, preferably of a dark color.

Mulberries in the Kitchen

Use the fresh berries right away or else freeze them because they don't store well.

- Protect the counter or table with plastic or paper towels or a clean cloth and pour the berries out into a single layer.

- Sort through the berries, discarding any stems or other foreign material as well as any bad berries.
- Rinse berries quickly in a colander—do not soak them in water because they'll lose juice.

Freezing Mulberries

DRY PACK: Just lay the berries whole in a single layer on a tray or jelly-roll sheet. When frozen hard, transfer the berries to freezer bags or containers. Seal, label and date, and return to the freezer.

OTHER: Mulberry butter and mulberry pies freeze well.

Eating Mulberries

Mulberries are delicious fresh or cooked.

Easy Mulberry Ice Cream

1. Place 4 cups mulberries in a food processor and puree. If desired, run puree through a sieve to remove seeds.
2. Add and blend together:

> 1/2 to 2/3 cup sugar
> I cup heavy cream
> I cup sour cream (NOTE: You can substitute plain or
>   vanilla yogurt for the cream and sour cream, if desired)
> I to 2 tablespoons cherry brandy or I 1/2 teaspoons vanilla

3. Pour the mixture into your ice-cream maker and follow the manufacturer's instructions.

Easy Mulberry Ice

1. Place 4 cups mulberries in a food processor and puree. Run puree through a sieve to remove seeds (optional, but recommended).
2. Add to the puree and thoroughly combine:

> 1/2 to 2/3 cup sugar
> I cup water

1 tablespoon lemon juice
2 tablespoons cherry brandy (optional)

3. Pour the mixture into your ice-cream maker and follow the manufacturer's instructions.

Mulberry Butter

1. Place 1 gallon fresh mulberries in a large saucepan or kettle.
2. Stir in ¼ cup water. Bring to a boil and quickly reduce the heat to
a simmer, stirring constantly.
3. When berries are broken up into pulp, remove from the heat and
run through a food mill or sieve to strain out the seeds. (If you
don't mind the seeds, omit this step.)
4. Return the puree to the stove and add the juice of 1 lemon plus 2
or 3 cups of sugar. Continue to simmer until thickened.
5. Cool and pour into freezer containers, allowing 1 inch of headspace
for expansion. Label, date, and freeze or refrigerate. Mulberry
butter is good with meats.

Old-Fashioned Mulberry Pie

A neighboring farmer says this is his favorite pie!
1. Combine:

4 cups fresh whole mulberries
¾ cup sugar
⅓ cup flour
1 tablespoon lemon juice

2. Place the mulberries in the bottom of an unbaked pie shell.
3. Dot the filling generously with pats of butter.
4. Top filling with crust and seal the edges. Prick top crust in several
places with a paring knife for ventilation. Lightly sprinkle crust
with sugar, if desired.
5. Bake at 400 degrees F about 35 minutes, or until the crust is lightly
browned.

171

Mulberry-Rhubarb Pie

Follow directions for Old-Fashioned Mulberry Pie, above, except use 2½ cups of mulberries and 1½ cups sliced rhubarb. Bake at 425 degrees F for about 40 minutes.

Mulberry-Cherry Pie

Follow directions for Old-Fashioned Mulberry Pie, above, except use 2 cups of mulberries and 2 cups cherries. Bake at 425 degrees F for about 40 minutes.

Sour Cream Mulberry Dessert

This recipe uses six individual dessert dishes that are ovenproof and that hold 1 to 1½ cups of liquid each. Custard cups are too small for these servings.

1. Place about ¾ cup mulberries in the bottom of each dessert dish. Sprinkle with a little lemon zest (optional, but tasty!).
2. Mix together:

> ½ cup sugar
> ½ cup brown sugar, packed
> ¼ cup flour
> I cup sour cream

3. Pour a scant ⅓ cup of batter over each dish of mulberries.
4. Bake for 30 minutes at 350 degrees F. Serve warm or cold.

PEACHES AND NECTARINES IN THE GARDEN

If you love the fresh peaches and nectarines you've purchased and ripened on the counter, just wait until you try one that's homegrown and tree-ripened! It's an unbelievably exquisite treat!

Nectarines are the bald cousins of peaches—they lack the fuzzy skin. Sometimes a peach tree will develop a branch of nectarines; sometimes a nectarine tree will grow a branch of peaches. Attractive, with dark, glossy foliage, both trees look alike and share the same growing conditions. Neither likes extremely cold winter conditions, with nectarines being less hardy than peaches.

Both peaches and nectarines need:

- a winter chill of at least 25 days under 45 degrees F (it varies by variety, however),
- a warm spring that allows blooming and fruit development without threat of frost,
- hot summers.

If this doesn't describe your area, take heart. If your climate is too warm, there are varieties that require low winter chill, made especially for you. If your climate is too cold, with protection, you can grow the cold-hardy varieties, or try growing them in containers, giving them their winter chill on an unheated porch or in a garage.

Description

Peaches and nectarines grow on trees. The flesh of the both fruits can be white or yellow.

Standard trees get about fifteen to eighteen feet tall, semidwarfs grow to eight or ten feet, dwarfs are six to eight feet tall, and genetic dwarfs (usually these are bushes) grow between four and seven feet tall.

Like apples, peaches and nectarines can have several different varieties grafted onto one tree. Unlike apples, which can be long-lived, peaches and nectarines have a shorter lifespan, perhaps living up to eighteen years.

LOCATION: Don't plant a peach or nectarine in the same place another one has grown—you'll risk insect and disease problems.

Since both peaches and nectarines are sensitive to cold, try to place them in a protected area. Planting the trees on a slope is ideal, to allow the cold air to flow and settle in lower areas. A slope also discourages standing water.

Peaches and nectarines can be container-grown in areas with severe winters. Select the dwarf varieties, which will get about five feet tall when grown in containers. You will have to move the trees so that they are below 45 degrees F for at least four hundred to six hundred hours in the winter. If necessary, you may have to hand pollinate the blossoms with a cotton swab.

GROWING RANGE: Although both peach and nectarine hybrids have been developed for the North, the best varieties can be grown only in zones 5 through 8 or maybe 9.

CHILL REQUIREMENT: From five hundred hours and up of temperatures under 45 degrees F, depending on variety, although a few hybrids have been developed that require only a few days of winter chill.

SOIL: The soil should be moist but well drained as peaches and nectarines both hate standing water. Till the area thoroughly, mixing in lots of well-rotted manure or compost, and sand, as needed, for drainage.

MOISTURE: Water, as needed, if you don't get at least one inch of rain each week the first year until frost.

LIGHT: Full sun.

PLANTING SEASON: Only in the spring, so that any bark damage has a chance to heal before winter.

HOW TO PLANT:

- Select one-year-old nursery stock that is still dormant or just beginning to bud.
- Place the tree at the same depth as it was growing at the nursery.
- Follow the steps in "Garden Notes" for planting fruit trees.
- Space standard and semidwarf peaches and nectarines fifteen to twenty feet apart, and dwarfs and genetic dwarfs six feet apart.
- Mulching the first year or two helps to preserve moisture and keep down weeds as the roots get established.

SUPPORT: None needed.

ONGOING CARE:

- Mulch to the drip line or till the area shallowly to keep the weeds down.
- Thin the fruit, because the weight of a full crop will damage the branch. Also, too much fruit results in poor size and flavor and depletes the tree's energy to the point of jeopardizing winter survival. The first thinning is the "June drop," when the unpollinated fruit falls off by itself. When the June drop is over, you can do additional thinning. Allow perhaps six inches between each fruit unless frost has killed part of the crop. In that case, it's okay to leave the fruit in clusters as long as the weight isn't too much for the branch.

PRUNING: The fruit develops on the new branch growth from the previous year. Once it's developed a fruit, that section of the branch will never bear again. If the tree is not pruned, the fruit will grow only at the branch tips, which keep getting longer and weaker. Pruning keeps the branches short and stocky, encourages new growth for fruiting, and allows sunlight to penetrate the interior of the tree. Pruning should be done as late in the spring as possible, but before blooming, so that the tree doesn't waste any energy on branches that are removed.

Starting when the tree is about five years old, prune:

- All the wood grown the previous two years.
- The main branches back by one third to one half to encourage side shoots.
- Side shoots more than two or three years old.
- Any weaker shoots, dead or damaged wood, etc.

For container trees, cut back the main branches by one third to one half. The tree will still bloom on new growth on the remaining branches.

Also, prune back the tree if frost killed the blossoms or if the branches winter-killed.

POLLINATION: Most peaches and nectarines self-pollinate, but it's good to have the help of bees.

WINTER PROTECTION: Protect the trees from wildlife, especially deer and rabbits.

PROPAGATION: Seeds, cutting, or, most commonly, grafting onto rootstock.

PEACH VARIETIES INCLUDE:
- **Reliance,** which will survive cold winters to –20 or –25 degrees F if protected, but can't take harsh winters. Reliance has showy flowers and medium fruit with bright yellow flesh. Zones 4–9.

- **Sunhaven** bears medium to large peaches with golden skin tinged with bright red. The sweet-flavored flesh is yellow-flecked and red and doesn't brown when exposed to air. Self-fertile. The tree may survive in zone 4, but it doesn't fruit when winter temperatures get below –19 degrees F. Zones 5–9.
- **Elberta,** my very favorite peach, is an old variety. The large richly flavored fruit has yellow flesh and the skin is golden with a red blush. Grown especially in Colorado and Utah. Excellent fresh, frozen, or cooked. Zones 5–9.
- **Red Haven,** which gets only twelve feet tall but spreads to eighteen feet. The yellow fruit is medium to large, very firm, and doesn't brown when exposed to air. Siberian rootstock gives it winter hardiness. Good fresh, frozen, or cooked. Zones 5–8.
- **Compact Redhaven** is a genetic dwarf that grows between six and ten feet tall, larger and hardier than other genetic dwarfs. It has the same fruit as Redhaven. Zones 5–8.

NECTARINE VARIETIES INCLUDE:

- **Mericrest,** which is the hardiest nectarine, has medium-sized red-skinned fruit with yellow flesh. Zones 6–9 and the southern parts of zone 5.
- **Red Gold** has large fruit with yellow flesh and bright-red, glossy skin. It has a distinctive flavor and is very aromatic. Very winter-hardy and resistant to spring frosts. The fruit stores well. The tree gets twelve to fifteen feet tall. Zones 6–8 and the southern parts of zone 5.
- **Sunglo** bears heavily and so must be thinned for best results. The medium-to-large fruit has skin that is golden orange and bright red and the flesh is deep yellow and firm. Hardy and vigorous. Zones 6–9 and the southern parts of zone 5.
- **Garden Beauty** is a genetic dwarf that grows about five feet tall and has lovely double flowers and fruit with red skin and yellow flesh. Self-fertile. Zones 6–9.

FRUITING: Peaches and nectarines bear fruit in one to three years.

YIELD: Dwarfs like Garden Beauty produce about one half to one bushel; the standards can produce two or more bushels.

HARVESTING: Picking the peaches or nectarines ripe from the tree gives you the very best flavor. The fruit doubles in size the last three weeks before harvest.

Ripe peaches smell great and taste good and sweet, and they don't have any green on the skin. If the peach also gives a little when you press the flesh with your thumb, it's ready to be harvested. Leave the fruit that doesn't pass all these tests to ripen a little longer on the tree.

To pick, twist the fruit and pull upward. Treat the fruit gently, as it is easily bruised. Don't leave any fruit on the ground, as it will attract insects that might then go to the tree.

If it's necessary, say when an early frost is on the way, you can pick the peaches partially green and ripen them in the house.

Peaches and Nectarines in the Kitchen

Peaches and nectarines can ripen on your kitchen counter, or, to hasten the process, place the fruit in a closed paper bag. Don't put unripe peaches or nectarines in the refrigerator because they won't be as sweet as if they were ripened at room temperature.

Once ripe, you can store the peaches in the refrigerator, buying yourself a few more days. Place the peaches or nectarines in a bowl or other container lined with a terry-cloth hand towel, and top the peaches with another towel—these will absorb moisture, which causes the peaches to rot, and they'll help protect the peaches from bruising. Never store peaches or nectarines in a sealed plastic bag or plastic container.

Since peaches and nectarines tend to ripen in a short span, and continue ripening after they're harvested, you will probably want a method to preserve your harvest. See "Kitchen Notes" for techniques for freezing pies, butters, etc. Or freeze peaches whole!

Freezing Peaches and Nectarines

DRY PACK: When they are ripe, place whole peaches in a sealed plastic bag and freeze in a single layer, if possible. (I usually can get nine large peaches in a zipper bag, and these will stack nicely and conserve space once they are frozen solid.) Label, date, and return to the freezer.

When it's time to use them, put the frozen peaches in a bowl of cold water for a few minutes and the skins will slide off easily in your hands. Remove the peeled peaches from the water immediately—if they are in the water too long, they will become soggy. Slice the peaches while they are still partially frozen and then use them as you would fresh peaches. Do remember to add a little more thickener (flour, corn starch, or tapioca) to the recipe if you use the frozen peaches for pies.

OTHER: Peach pie, sauce, butter, and dumplings all freeze well. As with apple dumplings, peach dumplings can be frozen unbaked and without the syrup and later, you can pull out the desired number of dumplings, add the syrup, and bake the frozen dumplings a little longer than usual.

Incidentally, peaches and nectarines are interchangeable in recipes, and the harvesting and storing directions are the same. For simplicity's sake, however, I'm referring only to peaches.

Eating Peaches and Nectarines

Of course, peaches and nectarines taste absolutely wonderful in their natural state! If you raise your own and do not use dangerous chemical sprays, just rinse them off and eat them fresh with their skins on because skins are nutritious.

NOTE: The flesh of most peaches and nectarines, when exposed to air, will turn brown. To avoid this, sprinkle with orange, lemon, pineapple, or lime juice or ascorbic acid, or dip into water with lemon juice in it.

Serving Ideas

- Fresh peaches can be halved and topped with a dollop of whipped cream, especially if cinnamon has been added (see "Kitchen Notes" section).
- Fresh peach slices can be sprinkled with a little sugar or honey to bring out their juice—this is the old farm technique that many still favor. Stir in a splash of dark rum, if desired.
- Peach slices tossed with grapes, strawberries, blueberries, kiwis, or other fruit make a delightful salad or dessert. Add a splash of lemon juice or apple juice to this mixture to keep peaches from turning brown.
- Try combining peach slices with orange slices and watermelon balls.
- Combine diced peaches with pineapple chunks and chopped celery.
- Peach slices make a nice salad with pear slices and red plum halves.
- Fresh sliced peaches are terrific topped with homemade vanilla or tapioca pudding. The pudding can be chilled or served still warm from the stove.

Easy Peach Ice Cream

1. Puree pitted peaches in a food processor to make 4 cups.
2. Add the following to the puree and blend in the food processor:

> 3/4 to 1 1/4 cups sugar (1 cup is good for peaches of average sweetness)
> 1 cup heavy whipping cream
> 1/2 cup of half-and-half (NOTE: You can substitute buttermilk or plain yogurt for the cream and half-and-half, if desired.)
> juice of 1 lemon
> 1/2 teaspoon almond extract

3. Pour the mixture into your ice-cream maker and follow the manufacturer's instructions.

Easy Peach Ice

1. Puree pitted peaches to make 4 cups.
2. Add the following to the puree and blend well in the food processor:

> 1/2 to 3/4 cup sugar
> 1 tablespoon lemon juice
> 2 tablespoons apricot brandy (optional)

3. Pour the mixture into your ice-cream maker and follow the manu-facturer's instructions.

Poached Peaches

1. Place 4 cups peach slices in a saucepan. (NOTE: Peeling is optional.)
2. Add: 1/4 to 1/3 cup sugar, 1 cup water, six whole cloves.
3. Bring just to a boil; then quickly reduce heat to a simmer. Cover and simmer 10 minutes or just until peaches are tender. Serve warm or chilled or freeze.

Easy Peach Butter

1. Make 4 cups peach puree (pit and quarter fresh peaches and puree in food processor)
2. Add to the puree:

> the juice and zest of 1/2 lemon
> 1/3 to 1/2 cup honey (TIP: Spray measuring cup with veg-etable oil coating; honey will pour out easily.)

3. Pour puree into a large skillet or other wide pan and place on the largest burner on the stove. Simmer on low, stirring often, until puree is thickened and reduced by about half, approximately 30 minutes.
4. Cool and pour into containers. Serve with bread, rolls, muffins, crackers, etc. Freeze or store peach butter in the refrigerator.

181

Old-Fashioned Peach Pie

1. Combine in a bowl:

> 5 cups peeled and sliced peaches
> 1/2 to 3/4 cup sugar
> 1 teaspoon lemon juice
> 1/3 cup flour (if freezing the unbaked pie, increase to 6 or 7 tablespoons)
> 1/4 teaspoon cinnamon

2. Pour fruit mixture into an unbaked pie shell.
3. Generously dot the filling with pats of butter. Sprinkle generously with cinnamon, if desired.
4. Top with crust and seal the edges. Prick the crust several times with a paring knife for ventilation. Lightly sprinkle the crust with sugar, if desired.
5. Bake at 400 degrees F about 40 minutes or until crust is lightly browned and peaches are tender when pricked with a paring knife. Serve warm or cold as is, or with a dollop of whipped cream or a scoop of vanilla ice cream.

Glazed Peach Pie

1. Bake and cool a pie shell.
2. In a saucepan, combine:

> 1 fresh peach, peeled, pitted, and well mashed or pureed
> 1/2 cup sugar
> 2 tablespoons butter
> 2 tablespoons cornstarch
> 1 cup water

3. Cook until thick and clear. Cool well.
4. Peel, pit, and slice about 3 cups of fresh peaches (about four large peaches).
5. To assemble the pie, place the peach slices in the pie shell and pour the cooled cooked mixture over them. Chill and serve with whipped cream, if desired.

Broiled Peaches

Halve and peel the peaches, removing the stone. Place them close together in an ovenproof pan with the rounded sides up. Broil on high about 3 inches from the heating element for 3 minutes. Turn peaches, sprinkle with ground cinnamon, and top each half with a pat of butter. Return to the broiler for another 3 minutes. Truly wonderful—and so fast and easy! If the peaches aren't very sweet or if you have a sweet tooth, you can drizzle honey over the cinnamon and butter before broiling the second time. Either method is great topped with cream or a dollop of whipped cream.

Easy Peach Dessert

1. Generously grease a 9 × 9-inch ovenproof pan.
2. Place 4 cups peeled and sliced peaches in the bottom of the pan.
3. Mix the following together and pour over the peaches:

> 2/3 to 1 cup sugar
> 1/4 cup flour
> pinch salt
> 1/2 cup sour cream
> 3 egg yolks

4. Bake at 375 degrees F about 30 minutes or just until the custard sets.
5. Serve warm or chilled with whipped cream or ice cream. Give the leftover egg whites to your cats, or use them to make a meringue. Be sure to refrigerate leftover dessert.

Easy Peach Cobbler

1. Melt 1/2 cup butter in a 2-quart baking pan in the microwave. Tip pan so butter coats the bottom.
2. Mix together in a bowl, then pour over the melted butter:

> 3/4 to 1 cup sugar
> 3/4 cup flour
> 3/4 cup cream
> 2 teaspoons baking powder

3. Mix together in a bowl, then pour over the batter:

>2 cups sliced and peeled peaches
>1/4 to 1/2 cup sugar
>juice and zest of 1 lemon
>1/4 teaspoon almond extract

4. Bake at 300 degrees F for 1 hour. The batter will rise to the top as it bakes. Serve as is or top with whipped cream or ice cream.

Easy Peach Fritters

A tasty breakfast treat!

1. Combine in a bowl and beat well:

>1 egg
>1/2 cup milk
>2 tablespoons melted butter

2. Add:

>1 cup flour
>2 tablespoons sugar
>2 teaspoons baking powder
>1/4 teaspoon salt

3. Slice 5 or 6 peaches and discard the pits. Stir the peaches into the batter.
4. Heat 1/3 cup vegetable oil in a skillet (using more, as necessary). Drop the batter-covered peach slices into the skillet one by one so that they aren't touching. Fry till lightly browned, then turn and fry on the other side. Remove to paper towels and sprinkle with confectioner's sugar. Serve warm.

Great Peach Dumplings

A family favorite!

1. Roll out one recipe of pie crust into a square or rectangle. Cut into squares large enough to wrap around each peach.
2. Use six or eight peaches, depending on size. Peel and halve each peach and remove the pit. Place the peach on a pastry square. Put 1 or 2 teaspoons sugar, a pat of butter, and a dash of cinnamon in the center of each peach where the pit used to be, and reassemble

the peach halves. Wrap the pastry around the peach, and seal. Place the wrapped peach with the cut pastry edges down in a casserole dish large enough to hold all the dumplings. Repeat with all the peaches. Sprinkle a little sugar on top of the dumplings.

3. In a saucepan, combine:

> 3/4 cup sugar
> 1 1/2 cups water
> 3 tablespoons butter
> dash cinnamon

4. Bring just to a boil; then remove from the stove.
5. Pour the liquid into the pan around the peach dumplings, being careful not to pour it directly over them.
6. Place the dumplings in the oven and bake at 425 degrees F for 35 minutes, or until the dumplings are lightly browned and the peaches are tender. Serve each dumpling with some of the syrup.

PEARS IN THE GARDEN

With my pine grove for protection against our harsh winters, I can grow fabulous pears that are larger, juicier, and better than any we've ever bought in a store. The upright trees have a nice oval shape, are very attractive in full leaf, and are positively glorious when in full bloom! Not only are pears delicious and beautiful, but they thrive even if they are neglected!

Pears are almost as hardy as apples, but they are a little more sensitive to weather. Wildly fluctuating spring temperatures might adversely affect pollination, and fluctuating fall temperatures might cost you the crop. Despite the occasional loss of a crop, pears are still worth raising, because when you do get fruit, the quality is outstanding!

Description

Pears grow on upright oval trees that have glossy leaves and lovely white blossoms. Standard trees grow to twenty feet; dwarf trees grow to only ten feet tall.

LOCATION: Pears will fit into any landscaping. Whether you have room for standards or dwarfs, or need to espalier a tree to fit a narrow space, you can find room for pears. If nothing else, they can be container-grown. Remember that you will need a pollinator.

GROWING RANGE: Zones 4 or 5 through 9.

CHILL REQUIREMENT: Many pears have a high chill requirement of at least eight hundred hours in temperatures under 45 degrees F.

SOIL: Pears prefer deep, well-drained soil. Pears can tolerate soggy soil better than other fruits, but for the good of the tree, it shouldn't be in standing water. If necessary, till in sand for drainage as you mix in well-rotted manure or compost.

MOISTURE: Pears need average moisture; more when the trees are getting established.

LIGHT: Full sun.

PLANTING SEASON: Spring.

HOW TO PLANT:
- Select nursery stock and get advice from the nursery about a pollinator.
- Follow instructions for planting fruit trees in "Garden Notes."
- Space standard trees about sixteen to twenty feet apart; space dwarfs about twelve feet apart.

SUPPORT: None.

ONGOING CARE: The fruit doesn't need thinning unless the weight risks damaging a branch.

PRUNING: Pears require little pruning. As the young tree grows, be sure that the developing branches are well spaced. After that, prune as required. Too much pruning is actually undesirable because it might invite disease.

POLLINATION: Pear trees need a pollinator, so you need at least two trees, or a nearby neighbor with a compatible pear tree. If you find yourself with only one tree and no pollinator, as I did when the other trees were destroyed in a storm, you can ask a friend for a blooming branch off their tree and place this in a bucket of water at the base of the tree. I quickly planted another tree, which had a few blossoms in the second year even though it was still quite small, and I did manage to get a harvest. Since three trees are even better than two for pollination, I've now added several more trees and look forward to lush harvests again.

WINTER PROTECTION: Defend the tree against wildlife, especially deer and rabbits.

PROPAGATION: From seeds or grafts onto rootstock.

VARIETIES INCLUDE:
- **Bartlett,** which has medium to large fruit that is yellow with a blush, and is sweet, juicy, and thin-skinned. Delicious fresh or cooked. Very popular. Zones 5–7.
- **Moonglow** has attractive fruit that's large, yellow, mild-flavored, soft, and juicy. It's a lovely upright, vigorous tree that produces fruit when very young. Disease resistant. Zones 5–8.
- **Bosc** produces large fruit with a long tapered neck, as is greenish yellow to brownish yellow with a cinnamon-colored wash on the skins. The flesh is crisp and a bit tart. Best eaten fresh. Keeps well. Zones 5–9.
- **Seckel** has small fruit with a brownish yellow to brownish red skin and flesh with a sweet and spicy flavor. Not the prettiest fruit, but the aroma and flavor beat out any other homegrown pear variety. Great fresh or cooked. Very hardy and very disease resistant. Zones 5–8.
- **Kieffer** produces medium to large, very sweet yellow fruit that has flesh with a gritty texture that makes it less favorable fresh but wonderful cooked. It keeps extremely well. Very disease resistant and very hardy. Doesn't require much winter chill, so it's good in warm climates. Good fresh or cooked. Tolerates heat and cold well. Zones 5–9.

FRUITING: Dwarf trees bear within two or three years, and standards bear at four or five years.

YIELD: Standard trees will produce five to ten or more bushels per year; dwarf trees yield about half a bushel of fruit.

HARVESTING: Pears are unlike other fruits because they should be picked when they are mature but not ripe. Leaving them to ripen on the tree causes them to develop gritty cells, and the fruit will be soft and be brown at the core.

Signs that the fruit is ready to harvest:

- The pear should be full sized.
- Usually the fruit is still green but has started turning yellow, although some varieties are red or russet-colored or blushed with red or pink.
- When tilted, the fruit will easily separate from the tree with its stem still attached. Be careful not to damage the fruit-producing spur.
- The flesh gets whiter.
- When you cut the fruit open, juice forms on the flesh.
- The seeds have turned dark.

Pears in the Kitchen

Pears can be ripened on the counter preferably at about 70 degrees F, or you can hasten the ripening by placing them in a paper bag with an apple.

NOTE: Pears ripen from the inside out, so don't wait until the outside is soft or the pear will be overripe mush. Check for ripeness by gently pressing on the stem end; if it gives a little, the pear is ripe.

You can store the unripe fruit in the refrigerator for a long time, sometimes even three months, and remove them when you want some to ripen on the counter. Never store pears in a plastic bag because it will make the flesh turn mealy.

Pears can also be wrapped in newspaper and kept in a cool cellar (about 40 degrees F) until ripened.

Freezing Pears

OTHER: I recommend that you do not freeze pears unless you've poached them or made them into puree, butter, or pie. Package well, seal, label, date, and freeze.

Eating Pears

Great eaten fresh, or they can be added to salads, compotes, etc. They are very good cooked in a variety of ways.

Serving Ideas

- For a simple salad, halve pears and serve on a bed of lettuce with a dollop of cream cheese, accented with fresh mint, if available.
- Toss fresh pear chunks with diced celery and nuts for a quick and easy salad.
- Combine pears with apples, celery, and nuts and toss with mayonnaise dressing for a Waldorf salad variation.
- Sprinkle fresh pear halves with orange juice and shredded coconut.
- Combine pear slices with peach slices and red plum halves.

Easy Pear Ice Cream

1. Place cored pears (with or without skins) in a food processor. Puree to make 3 cups. (NOTE: The ice cream will be smoother without the skins.)
2. Add the following to the puree and blend in the food processor:

    ½ cup sugar
    2 cups heavy cream (NOTE: You can substitute plain or
        vanilla yogurt for the cream, if desired.)

> 1 or 2 tablespoons lemon juice
> 1 teaspoon grated fresh gingerroot

3. Pour the mixture into your ice-cream maker and follow the manufacturer's instructions.

Easy Pear Ice

1. Place cored pears (with or without skins) in a food processor. Puree to make 4 cups. (NOTE: The ice will be smoother without the skins.)
2. Add the following to the puree and blend in the food processor:

> 1/2 to 3/4 cup sugar
> 1 or 2 tablespoons lemon juice
> 1 tablespoon grated fresh gingerroot or 1 tablespoon
>   cranberry liqueur or 1/4 teaspoon peppermint extract

3. Pour the mixture into your ice-cream maker and follow the manufacturer's instructions.

Poached Pears

1. Place 4 cups pear slices in a saucepan. (NOTE: peeling is optional).
2. Add: 1/4 to 1/3 cup sugar, 1 cup water, and 1 teaspoon lemon juice.
3. Bring just to a boil, then quickly reduce heat to a simmer. Cover and simmer 6 to 8 minutes or just until pears are tender. Serve with the liquid, warm or chilled, or freeze.

NOTE: Instead of the water, try poaching the pears in port wine or cranberry juice. Or use the water but add some creme de menthe for a green treat at Christmas time.

Easy Poached Pears with Almond Paste

Halve each pear the long way and peel and core each half. Place the halves in a covered saucepan with a little water. Gently simmer the pears until they are tender. Remove the pears with a slotted spoon and place a dollop of almond paste in each seed cavity. Serve warm.

Easy Pear Butter

A family favorite!

1. Clean, quarter, and core pears to make one gallon; peeling is optional. Puree pears with a food processor and place the puree in a large saucepan or place pear quarters in a large saucepan or kettle and puree them with the cordless blender.

2. Stir in:

> 1 cup pineapple juice
> ½ cup lemon juice
> ½ cup honey (TIP: Spray measuring cup with vegetable-oil coating first.)
> 2 teaspoons ground cinnamon
> ½ teaspoon ground cloves

3. Bring to a boil, then quickly reduce heat to a low simmer. Cook, stirring often, until somewhat thickened.

4. Cool and pour into freezer containers. Label, date, and freeze or refrigerate.

Old-Fashioned Pear Pie

1. Combine in a bowl:

> 4 cups peeled and sliced pears
> ⅓ to ½ cup sugar
> 1 tablespoon lemon juice
> ⅓ cup flour
> ¾ teaspoon ground ginger

2. Pour fruit mixture into an unbaked pie shell.

3. Generously dot the filling with pats of butter. Sprinkle lightly with cinnamon, if desired.

4. Top with crust and seal the edges. Prick crust several times with a paring knife for ventilation. Lightly sprinkle crust with sugar, if desired.

5. Bake at 400 degrees F about 45 minutes or till crust is lightly browned and pears are tender when pricked with a paring knife. Serve warm or cold as is, or with a dollop of whipped cream or a scoop of vanilla ice cream.

Sour Cream Pear Dessert

This recipe uses six individual dessert dishes that are ovenproof and that hold 1 or 1½ cups of liquid each. Custard cups are too small for these servings.

1. Slice pears to fill individual dessert dishes half full.
2. Mix together:

> ½ cup sugar
> ½ cup brown sugar, packed
> ¼ cup flour
> I cup sour cream

3. Pour a scant ⅓ cup of batter over each dish of pear slices.
4. Bake for 30 minutes at 350 degrees F. Serve warm or cold.

PLUMS IN THE GARDEN

If the only plums you have eaten fresh came from the grocery store, you might be tempted to pass up growing your own. This would be a big mistake! No matter where you live, some kind of plum has been adapted for your area.

Description

Plums are grown on trees. The fruit can be yellow, green, red, blue, or purple and is produced on spurs on the older branches, with the heaviest crop on wood that is two to four years old.

The standard trees are sixteen to twenty feet tall, the semidwarfs grow ten to twelve feet tall, and the dwarfs are usually six to eight feet tall.

LOCATION: Plums can be placed in an orchard, especially if planting several trees, or you can place them in the landscape as a grouping. Remember to check on the pollination needs of the varieties you select.

GROWING RANGE: There are varieties that can be grown everywhere. The dwarfs are the hardiest, because they are grafted onto sand cherry roots. The semidwarfs produce more fruit but are less hardy.

194

CHILL REQUIREMENT: From about five hundred to eight hundred hours of temperatures under 45 degrees F, depending on variety.

SOIL: Any deep, well-drained soil, although plums can take standing water better than most fruits. Till deeply and thoroughly and mix in lots of well-rotted manure or compost.

MOISTURE: One inch of water weekly until established. If the tree wilts, you'll lose the crop.

LIGHT: Full sun for the sweetest flavor.

PLANTING SEASON: Spring.

HOW TO PLANT:
- Select nursery stock and get advice about pollination.
- Plant the graft above the ground.
- Follow the steps in "Garden Notes" for planting fruit trees.
- Spacing varies greatly by variety; get good advice from your local nursery or Extension office.

SUPPORT: None.

ONGOING CARE:
- Keep the weeds from growing under the trees and competing with the feeder roots for water and nutrients. Mulching is the best way.
- Thin the fruit out so that it's about two inches apart. Do this after the June drop.
- Apply a layer of well-rotted manure one or two inches deep every spring.

PRUNING: Plums require little pruning. Just make sure the young tree develops a good branching habit that allows for good light and air circulation, and after that the tree is set. For bush plums, prune any shoots that have borne fruit for four years to encourage new growth.

Plums don't like to be trained, so if your space is limited, use a dwarf variety or consider the bush type as a hedge or as a container plant.

POLLINATION: Although some plums are self-fruitful, most require a second tree for pollination, and some even require a third tree.

WINTER PROTECTION: Defend the trees against wildlife, especially deer and rabbits.

PROPAGATION: Usually by grafting onto rootstock, because plums aren't true from seed.

VARIETIES INCLUDE:
- **Stanley**, a prune type that's a widely planted European plum that bears heavily. The large fruit has dark blue skin and yellow flesh and is sweet and richly flavored. Good fresh or cooked. Self-fertile. Zones 5–7.
- **Pipestone**, which has excellent-quality, large dark red-skinned fruit with yellow flesh. The skin is a bit tough. The tree is a little bigger than most plums. Vigorous and hardy. Good fresh or cooked. Zones 5–9.
- **Superior**, which was developed in Minnesota, has extra-large fruit with dark red skin that is easily peeled, if desired. The flesh is yellow and firm. Great fresh. Tree bears prolifically, even when young. Zones 5–9.
- **Toka**, also developed in Minnesota, has reddish orange skin and yellow flesh. The fruit has a rich, tangy-spicy flavor that's excellent. Good fresh and cooked. Very hardy. Zones 4 and 5.
- **Kaga** is a small plum tree. The medium-sized fruit has a strong, tangy flavor and is good eaten fresh or cooked. Zones 3 and 4.
- **Waneta** produces a heavy crop of large reddish purple plums with yellow flesh. Good fresh or cooked. Zone 3.

    NOTE: There are many kinds of plums available; it's important to choose the right plum for your area.

FRUITING: Usually begins three or four years from planting.

YIELD: Standards produce three to five bushels of fruit per tree, the semidwarfs yield between two and four bushels, and the dwarfs will bear one half to one bushel.

HARVESTING: The fruit is green until it's ripe. Then it might be yellow, red, or purple.

Harvest when the flesh gives just a little when pressed. It tastes best when picked fully ripened, but it will keep a little better if harvested just a little underripe.

To harvest plums, just twist off the fruit. The fruit will keep longer if it's harvested with the stem.

Plums ripen quickly, so be sure to check the tree daily. The plums that get the most sunlight ripen first—usually the fruit on top and toward the branch tips. All the fruit on the tree will be ripe within a week or ten days.

Plums in the Kitchen

Plums will store in the refrigerator for a week or two.

Freezing Plums

DRY PACK: Just place the whole, unpeeled plums into freezer bags. A single layer in a zipper bag conserves freezer space. Squeeze out as much air as possible, seal, label, date, and freeze.

SUGAR PACK: You can also freeze halved, sliced, or diced plums in sugar using 1 part sugar per 5 parts plums. Be sure to note the added sugar on the label in case you want to adjust any recipe you might be using.

OTHER: Stewed plums, plum sauce, plum pie, and plum butter also freeze well.

Eating Plums

All plums can be eaten fresh. Only the special varieties that have a naturally high sugar content can be dried into prunes; the others will spoil. Plums are great in salads or cooked or made into salad dressing.

Serving Ideas

- Pitted plums can be served sliced, with or without the skins. You can place them in a bowl with cream or milk poured over, and a sprinkle of sugar, if desired.
- Try combining plum halves with peach and pear slices.

Easy Plum Salad Dressing

1. Puree plums to make 2 cups.
2. Add ½ cup sugar and puree well.
3. Add one 8-ounce package of cream cheese and puree until smooth.
4. Chill and serve over fresh fruit.

Easy Plum and Rum Ice Cream

Absolutely wonderful!
1. Puree peeled and pitted plums in a food processor to make 1 cup. (Peeling is optional. To peel plums easily, dip plums into boiling water until skin splits, about 45 seconds, then plunge them in ice-water. Remove and peel.)
2. Add the following to the puree and blend in the food processor:

>   I cup heavy whipping cream
>   I cup sour cream
>   ½ to ⅔ cup sugar
>   I tablespoon dark rum

3. Pour the mixture into your ice-cream maker and follow the manufacturer's instructions.

Easy Plum Ice

1. Puree pitted, but not peeled, plums in a food processor to make 2 cups.
2. Add ½ cup water and place in a saucepan. Bring to boil, reduce heat, and simmer 5 minutes, stirring occasionally. Remove from heat.
3. Add ⅔ cup sugar and stir well to dissolve.
4. Stir in 1⅓ cups orange juice or white grape juice, and ½ teaspoon allspice or cloves or ¼ teaspoon of each.
5. Chill. (TIP: Place mixture in a large metal bowl in the freezer for a few minutes to cool it quickly.)
6. Pour the mixture into your ice-cream maker and follow manufacturer's instructions. Or, if you don't have an ice-cream maker, put the mixture in your freezer in the metal bowl and remove it after 15 minutes and beat it well. Repeat this several times until firm enough to serve.

Stewed Plums

Quick and easy, and so flavorful!
1. Place 2½ cups fresh plums that are halved and pitted, but not peeled, in a saucepan.
2. Add ½ cup water to the pan. Bring the plums to a boil; then reduce heat and simmer until nearly tender, about 3 minutes.
3. Add ⅓ cup sugar and simmer about 5 more minutes.
4. Serve warm or chilled. Refrigerate or freeze leftovers.

Plum Sauce

A bit fancier than stewed plums, this can be served as a dessert.
1. In a saucepan, mix together:

> 1 cup unsweetened apple juice (canned is fine)
> 1 tablespoon lemon juice
> ½ teaspoon cinnamon
> ⅛ teaspoon nutmeg

2. Add 3 cups fresh plum slices, pitted but not peeled. (The skins might come off somewhat, but I don't mind because they add color

to the liquid and are very tender, plus it saves time to leave them on.) Cook until plums are tender, about 5 minutes.

3. Serve warm or refrigerate or freeze.

Plum Butter

1. Place 6 cups plums, sliced and pitted, but not peeled, in a covered saucepan.
2. Add ¾ cup water. Bring plums to boil; then reduce heat, cover, and simmer about 5 minutes, until tender.
3. Stir in the following:

> 2 to 3 cups of sugar
> I tablespoon lemon juice
> I teaspoon cinnamon or allspice (optional)

4. Cook, uncovered, stirring often, until plum slices and skins become a smooth sauce. Continue to simmer a few minutes longer until reduced and thickened into fruit butter.
5. Use warm or chilled. Store in refrigerator or freeze.

Plum Pie

1. Combine the following:

> 4 cups sliced and pitted (but not peeled) plums, any
>   variety
> ½ cup sugar
> ⅓ cup flour
> ½ teaspoon cinnamon or allspice
> ¼ teaspoon almond extract (optional)

2. Place the plum mixture in an unbaked pie shell. Sprinkle plums with 1 tablespoon lemon juice. Dot liberally with butter.
3. Cover with the top crust and seal. Using the tip of a paring knife, prick five or six slits in the top crust. Sprinkle lightly with sugar, if desired.
4. Bake at 400 degrees F about 35 to 40 minutes, or until crust is lightly browned.
5. Serve warm or cold; alone or with cream, whipped cream, or ice cream.

RASPBERRIES IN THE GARDEN

I have delicious memories of helping my grandfather pick fresh raspberries, which we ate straight out of the bucket behind the barn.

Raspberries were planted along the edge of the farm grove, where they grew rampantly, renewing themselves by spreading where they wanted, unhampered by pruning or training to a support. This no-work method yields wonderful fruit and is the way nature intended raspberries to grow. However, it's not practical for the home gardener to allow the canes to grow at will across their lawns. So, this section will discuss how to grow "civilized" raspberries.

Description

Raspberries are produced on the canes of a perennial shrub plant. The fruit tastes sweet and tart at the same time, and the homegrown varieties are unsurpassed in freshness, flavor, and juiciness. Although at first glance, raspberries seem similar to blackberries, you can distinguish a raspberry from a blackberry because the white core of the raspberry remains on the cane when it's picked.

Raspberries can be red, purple, black, or golden. The red and yellow shrubs tend to be trailing, while the purple and black types are more upright. Each has their own taste, with golden raspberries said to have the richest raspberry flavor, and purple raspberries have the most juice. The black raspberry shrubs do not produce suckers.

LOCATION: When considering where to plant your raspberries, think in terms of hedges or groupings in the landscape. Raspberries tend to form thickets that would be good along a fence or property line. If space is an issue, you can train and prune the raspberries to take up less room but still produce good crops unmatched by anything you can buy.

NOTE: Do not plant red and black raspberries together, due to potential disease problems. Separate them by at least seven hundred feet. Also, do not plant raspberries near blackberries.

GROWING RANGE: If you can grow apple trees, you can grow raspberries. They like cold winters and a long cool spring.

Most varieties are for zones 4 through 8, although there are some for zone 3 and others that will go to zone 10, although many don't do well in warm climates. Black raspberries are more limited in their range because they prefer climates where peach trees grow well.

CHILL REQUIREMENT: About two hundred hours.

SOIL: Raspberries tolerate most soil types; even sand and clay will work just fine so long as you add organic material.

Fertilize well with two inches of rotted manure or use 20-21-20 fertilizer in early spring.

MOISTURE: At planting, water daily until the new buds open, then water once a week during the first growing season if you don't get an inch of rain. Raspberries have shallow roots, so the moisture needs to be at the surface.

LIGHT: Raspberries like full sun but can tolerate shade for part of the day. Red raspberries have the greatest need for full sun. Purple or black raspberries are the most tolerant of some shade, when planted on the east or west side of the house.

PLANTING SEASON: Spring, which is best in most areas, or fall. If transplanting suckers, do it in very early spring because they are ready to take off and grow.

HOW TO PLANT:

- If using nursery roots, place them in a bucket of water overnight. If transplanting suckers, drench them with water the day before planting.
- During planting, be certain the roots do not dry out.
- At planting, trim all the canes back to no more than eight to twelve inches.
- Avoid planting in areas infested with Canadian thistles or quack grass, unless these have been chemically destroyed at least several weeks prior.
- Till the planting bed thoroughly, incorporating well-rotted manure or compost.
- Space the plants up to three feet apart, or as close as one foot apart if making a hedge.
- If making rows, space the rows six or seven feet apart. One long, narrow row will produce more fruit than several closer rows.
- Place the plants two inches deeper in the ground than they grew in the nursery.
- Water thoroughly.

SUPPORT: Red or yellow raspberries that produce a single crop should be trellised. All the others may be given support, if desired. You can run wires on each side of the raspberry row and attach them to stakes at each end.

For even more control, you can make a clothesline-type trellis with rows of wire at about two feet and four feet above the ground, with the top wire spaced wider than the bottom. The fruiting canes are tied to these wires with cut-up pantyhose or cloth, never wire. The new nonfruiting canes are allowed to grow untied in the sunny centers until it's time to prune out the old canes, when they are lifted and trained in their place. This system makes it easier to harvest the berries.

ONGOING CARE:

- Remove all but four or five of the most vigorous canes the second spring.
- Mulch to retain moisture and hold down weeds.
- Till around the outside of the raspberry patch to discourage the suckers from spreading beyond the planting area.
- Weed carefully, because raspberries have shallow roots and suckers that could be damaged.
- Spray the plants with horticultural (dormant) oil in very early spring to prevent insect problems.
- Start a new patch elsewhere every few years because raspberries tend to go into a decline.

PRUNING:

- Cut off any winter-damaged tips.
- To save space, the canes can be maintained at four to six feet in length, but understand that this will reduce the crop, because you are removing the fruiting part.
- For black or purple raspberries, prune off about three inches from the tips of each cane when it reaches about two feet in height; this will stimulate the lateral branches and greatly increase the harvest.
- After the fruiting is over or it has been stopped by fall frost, cut the fruiting canes to the ground and start training the new canes. NOTE: For everbearing varieties, do not remove the canes until they've produced their second crop.

     NOTE: It's best to burn the canes you've pruned, to eliminate pests and disease.

POLLINATION: Raspberries are self-pollinating, but planting more than one variety enhances pollination. Also, it can extend the harvest season.

WINTER PROTECTION: Raspberries are very hardy and don't need winter protection unless the weather is extremely windy and cold and without snow cover for a long time.

     For protection, lay the canes down on the ground within the patch or the row, and pin down the canes that arch upward, being careful not to break them. Cover the canes with straw or mulch and then lay chicken wire over all to hold it in place. Be sure to uncover them again in early spring before any new growth has taken place.

PROPAGATION:

- Red raspberries multiply by sending out root suckers. Dig these out and transplant them to a new area in early spring or, in warm climates, in fall.
- Black or purple multiply by layering (rooting when the canes touch the ground). If you are going to do this, do not prune these canes. In late summer, pull back the mulch and pin the tips to the ground, perhaps covering them with a little soil or mulch. The next spring, dig and separate the new plants and transplant them elsewhere.

   NOTE: Don't dig or give away the suckers from patented plants.

VARIETIES INCLUDE:

- **Canby**, which bears a single crop of large, firm, midseason berries. The plants are semithornless. It's a personal favorite because the fruit is good fresh, cooked, or frozen. Zones 3–8.
- **Red Latham**, also a single-crop variety, is the most common red raspberry. Large, firm berries have a slightly tart flavor. Good fresh, cooked, or frozen—a favorite. Zones 3–8.
- **Bababerry** produces berries twice the size of other raspberries and it has limited chill requirements so it can be grown farther south than most varieties. Zones 4–10.
- **Kiwigold** is a delicious everbearing yellow-gold raspberry. Upright canes do not require staking. Zones 4–8.
- **Royalty Purple** is a cross between a red and a black raspberry. Zones 4–8.
- **Cumberland** is a single-crop black raspberry developed in 1896 and is still the most popular of the blacks, bearing large, firm, flavorful fruits. Zones 5–8.

FRUITING: Raspberries come into full fruit production the year after planting.

Everbearing raspberry varieties produce fruit on the end of new canes in the fall and then again in early summer the following year. In hot climates, you may not get the second crop.

Standard varieties, sometimes called single-crop raspberries, produce their fruit all at one time, usually in early summer.

YIELD: Perhaps one or two quarts or more of fruit per plant at maturity.

HARVESTING: Raspberries should be picked when they are full and round, and the fruit should be meaty with no dents. When ripe, the fruit will come off the core easily, without falling apart or going to mush (which means it's overripe). Be sure to keep up the harvest; check daily as the berries don't all ripen at once in the cluster.

Handle the delicate fruit gently. Use a broad container, as the weight of the berries could mash the lower berries in a deep bucket.

Raspberries should be refrigerated right away without prior washing. They are very perishable and should be used soon. If you have too many to use quickly, just freeze them or else cook them into sauce or butter.

Raspberries in the Kitchen

To use the fruit, pick them over carefully because the fruit is very fragile, removing any foreign matter, like leaves. Gently place raspberries in a colander and rinse with cold water. Lay on paper towels and gently pat dry.

Freezing Raspberries

If the raspberries have not been sprayed, freeze them unwashed. Otherwise, rinse quickly in a colander and pat dry.

DRY PACK: For loose fruit, freeze the raspberries whole on paper-towel-lined baking sheets. When frozen solid, place the loose berries in a freezer bag or container, with as little air as possible. Seal, label, and freeze.

If you don't mind that the fruit is frozen into a solid block, you can pack the unfrozen berries in containers. Before serving or using the raspberries in a recipe, you can partially thaw the block and break up the fruit with a fork.

SUGAR PACK: Some people like to freeze the berries with sugar, using ⅔ cup sugar per quart of raspberries. Put into freezer containers, seal, label, date, and freeze.

OTHER: Raspberries as butter, soup, pie, and sauce all freeze well.

Eating Raspberries

Raspberries are great fresh—in fact, at our house they might not make it back to the kitchen!

Strained raspberry puree can be added to lemonade, about 1 part puree to 4 parts lemonade. Garnish with fresh mint leaves, if desired.

Fresh raspberries are great served with champagne! The two complement each other. You can plop a few in a glass of champagne, or pour a little champagne over some raspberries in a bowl.

Raspberries can be added to salads, served with cream, or topped with whipped cream, and they are wonderful cooked.

Easy Raspberry Ice Cream

1. In a food processor, puree raspberries to make 2 cups. If you don't want to eat the seeds, run the puree through a sieve.
2. Combine the puree with:

> 2 cups buttermilk (or cream, or plain yogurt, or a combination of these)
> ⅓ to ½ cup sugar
> 2 or 3 tablespoons raspberry schnapps, curaçao liqueur, or rum (all optional)

3. Pour the mixture into your ice-cream maker and process according to the manufacturer's instructions.

Easy Raspberry Ice

1. In a food processor, puree raspberries to make 4 cups. If you don't want to eat the seeds, run the puree through a sieve and return to the food processor.
2. Add:

> ½ to 1 cup sugar
> the juice from one lemon
> ½ cup water

3. Puree the mixture and then pour it into your ice-cream maker and process according to the manufacturer's directions. Or, if you don't have an ice-cream maker, put the mixture in your freezer in a metal bowl and remove it after 15 minutes and beat it well. Repeat this several times until firm enough to serve.

Raspberry Champagne Ice

Place a heaping quart of raspberries in the food processor and add 1 cup of champagne and the juice of ½ lemon. Puree and pour into an ice-cream maker and process according to the manufacturer's directions.

Raspberry Sauce or Raspberry Butter

Place the fresh raspberries in a large saucepan and mash gently with a fork or potato masher. Add ½ to ¾ cup sugar per quart of raspberries, and bring to a boil. Reduce heat to a simmer and cook for a few minutes, stirring constantly. For raspberry butter, continue cooking a few minutes longer until somewhat thickened. To store, refrigerate or freeze.

No-Cook Raspberry Soup

1. In a food processor, puree raspberries to make 2 cups. Run the puree through a sieve to remove the seeds.
2. Blend in:

> ⅓ cup sugar
> ½ cup sour cream or plain yogurt
> 2 cups water
> ½ cup dry red wine (or substitute orange juice)

3. Chill and serve in small bowls.

Old-Fashioned Raspberry Pie

1. Place 4 cups raspberries in an unbaked pie shell.
2. Sprinkle fruit with 1 teaspoon lemon juice.
3. Combine in a small bowl and pour over the raspberries:

> ½ to ¾ cup sugar
> 1 teaspoon lemon juice
> ⅓ cup flour (if freezing the unbaked pie, increase to 6 or
>   7 tablespoons)

4. Generously dot the filling with pats of butter. Sprinkle with cinnamon, if desired.
5. Top with crust and seal the edges. Prick the crust several times with a paring knife for ventilation. Lightly sprinkle the crust with sugar, if desired.
6. Bake at 400 degrees F 40 to 45 minutes or till crust is lightly browned. Serve warm or cold as is, or with a dollop of whipped cream or a scoop of vanilla ice cream.

Raspberry Cream Pie

Follow directions for the Old-Fashioned Raspberry Pie, above, except pour 1 cup of heavy cream over the fruit after you place it in the pie shell and before you add the top crust.

Sour Cream Raspberry Dessert

This recipe uses six individual dessert dishes that are ovenproof and that hold 1 to 1½ cups of liquid. Custard cups are too small for these servings.

1. Place about ¾ cups of raspberries in the bottom of each dessert dish. Sprinkle with a little lemon zest (optional, but tasty!).

2. Mix together:

> ½ cup sugar
> ½ cup brown sugar, packed
> ¼ cup flour
> 1 cup sour cream

3. Pour a scant ⅓ cup of batter over each dish of raspberries.

4. Bake for 30 minutes at 350 degrees F. Serve warm or cold.

RHUBARB IN THE GARDEN

Rhubarb cheerily greets you in very early spring by starting new shoots even before the snow has all melted. Every farmer's wife had a rhubarb patch because she could run outside and quickly harvest some fresh stalks when she needed a dessert in a hurry. It's effortless to grow—and thrives despite total neglect! And it is one plant totally ignored by wildlife; animals won't eat the leaves or the stalks because they are too tart.

Rhubarb is the only vegetable that's used solely as a fruit in our diet. I've been astonished to discover friends who have never seen rhubarb, have never eaten it, and who have no idea how to cook with it, because it was such a common plant in my childhood. Although not a true fruit or berry, rhubarb is used like fruit to make butters, sauces, and pies, and it's often cooked with other fruits, so I'm including it here.

Description

Rhubarb is a perennial plant that you start from a root crown. The part that is eaten is the leaf stalk. The stalks of the older rhubarb varieties were mainly pale green tinged with red on the outside, and pale green on the inside. These varieties were very tart and required a lot of added sugar. Newer hybrids are a very pretty bright red inside and out and are sweeter, requiring much less sugar in cooking.

When I started my rhubarb patch, I planted six crowns; for most families, I suggest planting only two, which will probably supply you with more rhubarb than you can ever use.

NOTE: Both the roots and the leaves are poisonous.

LOCATION: The two- to three-foot-tall plant is attractive and could easily be planted in landscaping or a flowerbed. The leaves are quite large, like giant green hearts, and have a tropical look.

GROWING RANGE: Zones 3 through 8, perhaps even extending into zone 2 with winter protection. Rhubarb prefers to grow in the north half of the United States. In warmer climates it sometimes can be grown through the winter as an annual, or sometimes it will go dormant through summer.

CHILL REQUIREMENT: Rhubarb needs at least two months of winter chill. The top two to three inches of soil should freeze solid for best results.

SOIL: Almost any kind of deep soil suits rhubarb so long as the roots aren't soggy or in standing water. Add lots of well-rotted manure or compost if your soil is poor.

MOISTURE: Average. After the plants are established, rhubarb will seldom need watering, except in hotter, dryer areas.

LIGHT: Full sun to light shade.

PLANTING SEASON: Early spring. In warm climates, plant in the fall.

HOW TO PLANT:
- I recommend selecting the newer high-sugar hybrids from nurseries, or get a crown and root from a friend.
- Plant the crowns before they've developed shoots, if possible.
- Thoroughly and deeply till the planting area, mixing in well-rotted manure or compost.

- Position the crowns in the ground so that the roots go down and the crown goes up, and place the crown 2 or 3 inches below the soil surface.
- Space the crowns 3 or 4 feet apart in each direction.
- Water and mulch the first season.

SUPPORT: None.

ONGOING CARE: Once established, rhubarb needs almost no attention! It doesn't need any mulch, and it doesn't require weeding. The gigantic leaves shade the crowns and the ground near the crowns, so weeds will not start.

You can apply some well-rotted manure on top of the plants before they begin growing in early spring if your soil is poor or the plant doesn't look vigorous.

In hot weather, rhubarb tends to go to seed (except the hybrids, listed below). Although the airy white fronds are quite attractive above the dark green leaves, these seed stalks should be pruned out for the good of the plant.

Every eight to ten years, you're supposed to dig up the rhubarb to divide the crowns, to keep the plants vigorous and the roots uncrowded. I've never known a farmwife who did this, and the plants continue to do just fine, perhaps because we have such rich soil. If your soil is poor or your rhubarb plants look like they're in decline, you might consider dividing the crowns. This should be done in very early spring, retaining as many of the roots as possible and leaving at least two "eyes" per four- to six-inch cluster for new shoots. After dividing them, you'll have to wait for harvest just the same as you did for a new planting.

PRUNING: Not necessary.

POLLINATION: Not necessary.

WINTER PROTECTION: Not necessary; just leave the collapsed leaves in place till spring. If you live in an exceptionally cold area, you might want to add a thick layer of mulch for additional protection.

PROPAGATION: From root division. Although you can start rhubarb from seeds, it's not recommended as the plants won't be true.

VARIETIES INCLUDE: NOTE: Be sure to check with your local Extension before growing rhubarb if you live in the southern half of the United States.

- **Chipman's Canada Red,** which requires less added sugar because it's naturally sweeter than other varieties. The stalks are bright red, inside and out, and give a nice color to recipes. It rarely goes to seed and is a prolific producer. Highly recommended!
- **Crimson Red** is another excellent hybrid that has a wonderful flavor and is sweeter than most. Produces lots of plump stalks that are bright red in color.
- **McDonald's Canadian Red** has stalks that are dark red inside and out and naturally sweet. The skins are tender and never need peeling.
- **Valentine** has thick stalks with deep red flesh that is very sweet and flavorful. It doesn't develop seed stalks and produces quickly.

FRUITING: You can have a light harvest in the second year, and then you can harvest the rhubarb at will, but never more than half the plant at one time.

YIELD: Five pounds per mature plant.

HARVESTING: Do not harvest any rhubarb the first year. The second year, harvest should be light to allow the plant to get established.

After the third year, take all you want as long as you leave half the leaves to benefit the roots.

The mature plant will spread to three or even four feet in diameter, so it's unlikely that you'll ever come close to harvesting half of it! I have so much that I give it away by the armload.

How to harvest: Just grab the twelve- to twenty-four-inch-long stalk over halfway to the ground with both hands, and pull up and a little to one side. When I harvest rhubarb, I take a knife to the garden to cut off the leaves, which can be laid on the ground around the plants to return nutrients to the soil.

The first pickings in late spring are the most tender; however, I harvest rhubarb as I need it all summer long. The narrower stalks found more toward the center of the crown usually have the most delicate flavor. The larger, thicker outer stalks are great in spring, but by summer they might become tough or stringy, especially in hot weather, but they'll cook up fine if you've planted one of the hybrid varieties. If necessary, you can peel these older stalks, but I don't bother. If they're so tough you can't cut them easily with a paring knife, just discard them and get more. After all, rhubarb produces abundantly, once established, and you'll likely have more than you can possibly use.

Rhubarb in the Kitchen

The fresh stalks (minus the leaves) will keep for two or three weeks in the refrigerator—but why bother, when you can just step outside and harvest some more?

Freezing Rhubarb

DRY PACK: Just cut off the leaves and ends, rinse off the stalks, trim any blemishes, and chop into quarter-inch or half-inch slices. Place premeasured amounts in freezer bags, squeeze out any excess air, label and date, and freeze.

It's ready to use in your favorite recipes, and you don't even have to thaw it first. If you need it to be loose, say as a fruit addition to muffins, just pound the bags with the flat side of a meat mallet to break apart the chunks.

SUGAR PACK: Some people prefer to freeze rhubarb with sugar, using 1 part sugar per 4 parts rhubarb (perhaps a bit less, if using a high-sugar-content variety). Be sure to note that it's packed in sugar on the label.

OTHER: Rhubarb cooked as sauce or butter or baked in pies also freezes well.

Eating Rhubarb

Rhubarb is one thing you don't want to eat raw, although most farm children have tried it and some even develop a taste for the tart stalks.

Keep in mind that the leaves are poisonous, so don't allow children to eat even a little. Don't toss the leaves over the fence to the pigs, either, although they do like the stalks.

NOTE: Always cook rhubarb in nonreactive cookware; stainless steel is excellent. Never use aluminum.

TO PREPARE RHUBARB FOR COOKING: Cut off the leaves and the whitish root ends of the rhubarb stalks. Inspect each stem and cut off any possible insect damage. Wash the stems in cool water, but do not soak the rhubarb, as it will take on liquid. Slice the stalks crosswise into chunks, perhaps half an inch long.

I couldn't resist giving you several recipes for rhubarb pie—after all, it was called "pie plant" by the early settlers.

Easy Rhubarb Ice Cream

Delicious!

1. Combine:

> 2 cups sweetened rhubarb sauce (see below)
> 1/3 to 2/3 cup additional sugar
> 2 cups heavy cream or 1 cup cream and 1 cup sour
>   cream or substitute plain vanilla yogurt for the
>   cream and sour cream, if desired
> 3 tablespoons whiskey (optional)

2. Place the mixture into your ice-cream maker and follow the man-ufacturer's instructions.

Easy Rhubarb Ice

1. Combine:

> 2 ½ cups sweetened rhubarb sauce
> ½ to ¾ cup additional sugar
> 1 ¼ cups cranberry juice
> 3 tablespoons whiskey (optional)

2. Place the mixture in your ice-cream maker and follow the manufacturer's instructions.

Easy Rhubarb Sauce

A traditional dish prepared by farmwives for generations.

1. Cut the stalks into ½-inch segments or run them through a food processor using the thickest blade. Weigh the rhubarb and make a note of the weight.
2. Place the rhubarb in a saucepan with a little water, perhaps enough to come to a depth of ¼ inch on the bottom of the pan. Cover and simmer until the rhubarb is tender, stirring occasionally. Remove the lid and continue simmering until the rhubarb chunks start to break up.
3. Add sugar to taste—starting with about ⅓ cup per pound of rhubarb. Stir well and simmer a few minutes longer, until the sugar is completely dissolved in the sauce. NOTE: the cooked sauce tastes much sweeter after it cools—it is easy to add too much sugar. The warm sauce should taste a bit tart.
4. Serve warm or chilled in bowls, or use as a sauce over vanilla ice cream or shortcake topped with whipped cream.

    NOTE: For a tasty variation, add flavored gelatin (try strawberry, raspberry, or peach) to the sauce with the sugar, perhaps 1 tablespoon per each ⅓ cup of sugar. As a bonus, the gelatin also tints the rhubarb, which can appear a bit bland unless you've planted a hybrid variety.

Easy Rhubarb Butter

Follow instructions for Rhubarb Sauce, above, but simmer it a few minutes longer until thickened. You might want to increase the sugar a bit.

Easy Rhubarb-Cherry Jam

1. Simmer together for 20 minutes:

> 6 cups thinly sliced or chopped rhubarb (run rhubarb
> through the thin blade on a food processor)
> 3 to 4 cups sugar
> 1 can cherry pie filling

2. Add one 3-ounce box of cherry gelatin. Stir together, then remove the jelly from the stove and cool. If desired, briefly blend it in a food processor. Store in the refrigerator or freeze.

Easy Rhubarb Pie

This recipe is very old!
1. Line pie tin with pastry and fill with chopped rhubarb.
2. Whisk together:

> 1 cup sugar
> 1 cup cream
> 2 large egg yolks
> 1/4 cup flour
> pinch of salt

3. Pour the cream mixture over the rhubarb and bake at 350 degrees F for about 40 minutes or until the top is lightly browned and the rhubarb feels soft when a paring knife is inserted into the pie.

Mom's Old-Fashioned Rhubarb Pie

1. Mix together in a bowl and then pour into an unbaked pie crust:

> 4 cups rhubarb, cut into 1/2-inch lengths
> 3/4 to 1 1/2 cups sugar (depending on how naturally sweet
> or tart your rhubarb is, as well as your taste preference)
> 1/4 cup flour, slightly heaping
> pinch of salt
> 2 eggs, slightly beaten
> 2 tablespoons rum (optional, not part of Mom's original
> recipe)

2. Sprinkle the filling generously with cinnamon; dot it liberally with butter.

3. Top with crust and seal the edges. Prick crust several times with a paring knife for ventilation. Lightly sprinkle the top crust with sugar, if desired.

4. Bake at 400 degrees F for 40 minutes or until rhubarb is tender and crust is lightly browned. Serve warm or cold, plain or with whipped cream or ice cream.

Quick and Easy Rhubarb Pie (one crust)

1. Place 4 cups diced rhubarb in the bottom of an unbaked pie shell.

2. Sprinkle one 3-ounce package of strawberry gelatin over the rhubarb.

3. In a bowl, combine:

> 3/4 cup sugar
> 1/2 cup flour
> 3/4 teaspoon ground cinnamon
> 1/4 cup melted butter

4. Sprinkle flour mixture over the rhubarb.

5. Bake at 350 degrees F for 50 minutes until rhubarb is tender and topping is lightly browned. Serve warm or cold with strawberry ice cream or whipped cream, if desired.

Old-Fashioned Strawberry-Rhubarb Pie (two crust)

A family favorite!

1. Combine in a bowl:

> 2 cups strawberries, hulled and cut in half
> 2 cups rhubarb, cut into 1/2-inch lengths
> 2/3 to 3/4 cup sugar
> 1/3 cup flour
> pinch salt

2. Pour fruit mixture into an unbaked pie shell.

3. Generously dot the filling with pats of butter. Sprinkle generously with cinnamon.

4. Top with crust and seal the edges. Prick crust several times with a paring knife for ventilation. Lightly sprinkle crust with sugar, if desired.
5. Bake at 400 degrees F about 45 minutes or till crust is lightly browned and rhubarb is tender when pricked with a paring knife. Serve warm or cold as is, or with a dollop of whipped cream or a scoop of vanilla ice cream.

Mom's Whipped Rhubarb Pie

A childhood favorite!
1. Combine in a saucepan and simmer until the rhubarb turns to sauce, about 5 minutes:

> 2 cups sliced rhubarb
> ⅔ cup sugar
> 1½ cups water

2. Add one 3-ounce package of strawberry or raspberry gelatin and stir until dissolved.
3. Chill until mixture is syrupy.
4. Whip 1½ cups heavy cream and 1 tablespoon powdered milk until stiff.
5. Fold chilled rhubarb mixture into the whipped cream.
6. Pour into baked pie shell or graham cracker crust and chill in the freezer. Serve partially frozen

Easy Rhubarb Dessert

1. Place 5 cups of rhubarb cut into ½-inch slices in a greased 9 × 12-inch pan.
2. Sprinkle rhubarb with:

> 1 tablespoon quick tapioca
> one 3-ounce package of strawberry gelatin
> 1 cup sugar

3. Top with 3 cups miniature marshmallows.
4. Bake at 350 degrees F for about 1 hour. Serve warm with whipped cream.

Baked Rhubarb and Orange Sauce

So easy, and you can bake it right along with a roast or chicken!

1. Combine in an oven-proof casserole:

> 4 cups rhubarb, cut in 1/2-inch slices
> 2 oranges, peeled and cut into chunks or 1/2 cup orange
> concentrate
> 1 cup sugar
> dash salt
> 12 cloves, tied in cheesecloth
> 2 cinnamon sticks, 2 inches long

2. Cover and bake for 1 hour at 350 degrees F. Remove cloves and cinnamon and serve warm or chilled.

Rhubarb Cobbler

Absolutely wonderful! For company, I double this in my large spatter-ware roasting pan.

1. Place 3 or 4 cups diced rhubarb in the bottom of a 9 × 9-inch pan.
2. To make biscuit dough, cream together ¾ cup sugar and 3 tablespoons butter. Stir in:

> 1 cup flour
> 1/2 cup buttermilk (can substitute milk)
> 1 teaspoon baking powder
> 1/2 teaspoon orange extract
> 1/4 teaspoon salt

3. Spoon the biscuit dough over the rhubarb.
4. To make the topping, combine:

> 1/2 to 1 cup sugar
> 1 tablespoon cornstarch
> 1/4 teaspoon salt

5. Sprinkle the topping over the rhubarb. Pour 1 cup boiling water over all.
6. Bake at 375 degrees F for 1 hour. Serve while still warm, with whipped cream or milk, if desired.

STRAWBERRIES IN THE GARDEN

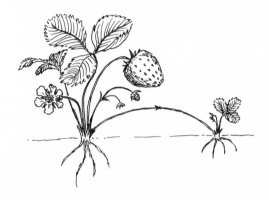

Just the thought of tender, juicy strawberries bursting with flavor makes most mouths water. Yet the only way you'll get this treat is if your strawberries are homegrown, because the store-bought varieties are hard, dry, and have very little flavor.

The most important thing to remember about strawberries is that their crowns and roots cannot bear to be in standing water or soggy soil. Even so, they will need a steady supply of moisture.

Strawberries are so versatile, you can plant them in their own beds, in containers on your patio, mixed in a flower garden or box, or even as a ground cover around shrubs in your landscaping—although they will produce less abundantly if they don't get a full day's sun.

Strawberries are easy to grow anywhere. If you choose the right varieties, you'll get luscious fruit the very first season.

Description

Strawberries grow on perennial plants only six to ten inches tall. Strawberry plants come in many varieties, and each has special qualities: maybe it produces fruit extra early, it might tolerate cold or drought, the berries might freeze especially well, or maybe it's resistant to a particular disease.

There are three main types of strawberry plants commonly grown by the home gardener:

- **Junebearing**, which bear large crops all at once in June, were the traditional choice for farmwives, so they could get the canning over with before the really hot weather in July or August.
- **Everbearing** strawberries produce a moderate crop in June or July with a second, smaller crop later in the summer. Everbearers produce very well in the long days during Alaska's summers. They grow best in areas that have cool weather in late summer. Since my summers are usually hot, I've always gotten more total fruit with the Junebearing, so have favored them until recently.
- **Day-Neutrals** are the newest type and are supposed to be true everbearers, fruiting steadily from spring through fall, except during the hottest weather of the summer in July. I've switched over to all day-neutral plants.

LOCATION: If possible, don't plant your strawberries where they grew for the previous two years, or where you've recently grown tomatoes, peppers, or potatoes. For convenience, plant them where you can water them easily and often, if necessary.

One way to fit them into your yard is to edge your landscaping with a row of strawberries. To add zest, try a second row of brightly flowered dianthus to contrast its grayish mossy leaves with the vivid green of the strawberries. Another excellent flower to mingle with strawberries is the Carpet of Snow alyssum, which is covered with tiny white flowers from early summer through later fall, surviving frost. The alyssum is shorter than the strawberries, so I recommend planting them in front of the strawberry row. Or you can alternate them, planting one strawberry plant, one flower seedling, etc.

GROWING RANGE: Strawberries can be grown anywhere, so long as you select the right varieties for your area.

CHILL REQUIREMENT: Between one hundred and three hundred hours below 45 degrees F, depending on the variety.

If you live in the South and don't have cool winter days, you can dig up the daughters and place them in vented plastic bags (buy these or punch holes yourself) in the refrigerator. Or you can replant your patch every year from roots that were prechilled for you by the nursery.

SOIL: Any fertile, well-drained soil. If your soil isn't well drained, be sure to blend in some sand for good drainage. Till thoroughly and mix in lots of rotted manure, compost, or peat moss.

The manure or compost should do it, but if you find you need fertilizer, there are blends made especially for strawberries. Don't go overboard, because too much fertilizer gets you lots of big green leaves and only a few small berries without much flavor.

MOISTURE: Strawberries have shallow roots that go down less than six inches, so be sure that plants get at least one inch of water per week, and even more in really hot weather or if the plants are in a container. Drip irrigation is the first choice; overhead sprinkling will work also if you do it in the early morning so the plants dry off fairly quickly.

LIGHT: At least six hours of full sun daily. They'll tolerate less, but the size of the crop will be reduced.

PLANTING SEASON: Early spring for most of the northern half of the United States, or late winter for most of the South and California.

HOW TO PLANT: Buy dormant plants that are certified to be disease-free from a reputable nursery.

NOTE: Before you begin to plant your strawberries, it's important that you understand the plant physiology. Strawberries don't have a single stem with leaves and branches growing out of it, like most plants. Strawberry leaves grow out of a small thick area at ground level, called a crown. The roots grow out of the base of the crown, up to six per leaf. New leaves create new roots. The crown is very particular about how high or low it is planted in the ground, and the plant will die if it's not placed correctly.

PLANTING METHODS: You'll probably be buying dormant strawberry plants that are tied together in a bunch. It's best to plant them as soon as they arrive, or you can store them in the refrigerator for a short time. The roots should not be exposed to the sun or to drying winds, so try to plant them on a calm, cloudy day and keep the strawberries covered with a damp cloth until they are in the ground. If the roots die, the leaves can't form.

Strawberry crown

To prepare the planting bed, thoroughly till the entire area to loosen the soil, and blend in the sand and manure or compost.

To plant the strawberries, many people will tell you to dig a hole, mound dirt in the bottom, drape the roots over the mound and cover the plant with soil to the crown. This is difficult and takes more time than is necessary, especially if you're planting fifty or a hundred strawberries.

With my method, your strawberries will be planted faster and more accurately than with the mound method. Here's how:

- Prune the roots to six inches long.
- Slice a hand trowel in the prepared soil, making a slit two or three times as wide as the trowel and as deep as the bare roots.
- Insert the roots, fanning them out in the slit.
- Position the plant so that the crown top is one third above the soil line and two thirds below.
- Carefully hold the plant in this position with one hand, and use the other hand to press the slit closed.

When all the strawberries are in the ground, water them well and then check that the crowns are still positioned so that they're barely above the soil line; too high or too low, and they will die. Also, check that all the roots are in the ground and covered by earth.

BEDDING METHODS:

The Strawberry Patch. This is a solid bed of strawberry plants. You start it by spacing the crowns two feet apart in all directions. The plants are allowed to send out runners until the bed is a mass of strawberries growing everywhere.

Weeding is hardest with this method. In theory, the thick mass of strawberries supposedly chokes out a lot of weeds (not true on our farm!) and produces the most crop in the space. However, the berries get smaller as the plants get crowded. And the patch will have to be completely replanted every four years or so to maintain vigor.

If you choose this method, I strongly recommend preemergence weed control (see "Weeding" in "Ongoing Care").

The Alternating Row. This method renews the bed without ever buying new plant stock.

To start, you plant strawberry crowns about one foot apart in rows about four or five feet apart. Be sure to stake the original rows so that you will keep track of which plants are the oldest. The runners are allowed to grow, and you should remove or redirect those that are too close together.

By the third year, the berries will be a mass bed.

In the fourth year, move the stakes about one or one and a half feet over and till under the strawberries in the original rows in a swath about one and a half feet wide, leaving all the rest. As you are tilling, mix in lots of well-rotted manure. The daughters from the original plants will send runners back into the cleared row, or you can transplant daughters from other plants.

The fifth year, move over another one and a half feet and repeat the process for the fourth year, adding manure as you till under another swath beside the original row (these are second-year daughters).

Continue this process, each year tilling about one fourth of the patch and allowing the remaining plants to send runners into the tilled row— or remove the rooted daughters and plant in the newly tilled rows.

The Moving Row. This is a simpler version of the alternating row method. Plant a single row of strawberries, one foot apart, on one edge of your vegetable garden. Allow this row to move across the garden, by directing the runners all in the same direction, or else by removing the runners from one side of the row and allowing them to grow on the other side. Starting the fourth year, till under one foot of strawberries on the oldest side. When the strawberry row reaches the other end of the garden, transplant the rooted daughters to the other side and start over.

The Strict Row. In this system, the strawberry plants aren't allowed to spread; the daughters are removed and planted elsewhere or discarded. The strawberries remain in neat rows that are easily cultivated, and the plants are replaced in their fourth season.

Weeds are easily controlled with minimal hand pulling. A tiller does most of the work if the strawberries are planted about one foot apart in two-foot rows, or whatever width accommodates your tiller.

B.W.T. (Before I got my Wonderful Tiller), I maintained a strict-row bed by keeping the rows mulched with straw and removing daughters to create new rows. The downside was that the plants started later in the spring, because the mulch insulated the ground and kept it from warming up, unless I went to the trouble of removing all the mulch—which was a lot of work in my large bed. Using a tiller is far easier.

The Pyramid Method. With this method, you can plant fifty crowns in a tiered area only six feet wide. It looks nice, weeding is minimized, and harvest is easy because the beds are raised and always within a three-foot reach. This method was especially developed for people with very little space. To make your pyramid:

- Use 2 × 6-inch redwood or cedar planks to make 2-, 4-, and 6-foot squares, or you can order a kit that uses precut corrugated

metal strips for round tiers. Kits can include a buried sprin-
kler system as well as supports for netting to keep the birds
out of the berries and to hold straw or leaves over the pyramid for overwintering.

- Starting at ground level, lay down the six-foot tier and fill it
with topsoil mixed with sand and peat and some rotted
manure, if you have it. Tamp the soil down well before starting
the next tier, to prevent problems with settling. Center the
four-foot tier on top of the six-foot tier, fill it with the same soil
blend, and tamp it down well. Repeat the process with the two-
foot tier on the very top, and you'll have three planting levels.
- By spacing the plants about nine inches apart, you can get
fifty strawberries in three round tiers as follows:
    —Seven plants in the top two-foot tier, placing one in the
    center and six in a circle
    —Seventeen plants in the middle four-foot tier
    —Twenty-six plants in the bottom six-foot tier
- To plant the strawberries, use your hand trowel to make
slits, as described above in "Planting Methods," but have the
slits all point to the center of the pyramid so that the roots
won't be overlapping.
- Mulch all the tiers to help retain moisture. You can use peat
moss for this, at least until the strawberry plants leaf out,
when you can add regular mulch. Don't place the mulch over
or close to the crowns, to prevent them from rotting.

The soil in the pyramid dries out more than that in a ground-level
bed, so it will have to be watered at least once or twice a week during
hot weather, unless you get good rains.

Since the strawberries are so close together, you will have to be more
diligent about fertilizing and might want to use a commercial blend.

Any daughters will have to be removed, since the plants are
already so close together.

After the first hard frost, spread straw or leaves or other loose
mulch over the berries and cover with netting to keep it in place. To
further prevent winter damage, you might want to lay eight inches of
mulch right up to the lowest tier wall.

After danger of a hard frost the next spring, remove the netting and the straw. Water and fertilize the plants and you'll have a bountiful fruit harvest.

The fourth year, replace the crowns with new plants and start over.

A Strawberry Tub or Barrel. This allows a berry harvest even on a sunny balcony or deck. Strawberries are planted every six inches or so all around the sides of the planter in holes that are about an inch and a half across. You can purchase a ready-made planter, which usually has a lip at the bottom of each hole to prevent the water and soil from spilling out. Or, you can make your own using a wooden barrel or chemical-free container:

- Make a watering tube from PVC pipe drilled with small holes. This is placed down the center of the tub before filling it with soil. The pipe should be long enough to protrude two or three inches above the soil line.
- Drill two or three holes in the bottom of the tub and mount the tub on three or four bricks or cement blocks. This allows for drainage and also will minimize water stains on your deck or patio.
- Cut a piece of black landscaping cloth to cover the holes. This allows water to filter out the bottom, keeping the dirt inside. Top the cloth with a couple of inches of pebbles or sand, insert your PVC pipe, and then you're ready for soil.
- Blend good topsoil with sand and peat, as with the pyramid method.
- Plant the strawberries from the bottom of the container up, adding soil in layers so that you can reach inside to spread out the roots as you go. The crowns must not be below the dirt level, nor should they be too high—check this carefully.
- Water and fertilize the same as with the pyramid method, but check more frequently to ensure that the barrel doesn't get too soggy or too dry.
- Remove all runners, or set a small pot under them and then cut them off when they're well rooted.

Flowerpots or Window Boxes. Using these, you can grow strawberries indoors in a sunny window, and they will fruit. Here's how:

- Choose a container that's at least six inches deep.
- Place the container on a tray filled with pebbles to allow drainage.
- Line the bottom with landscaping fabric or quality paper towels to filter the draining water, keeping the soil in the pot.
- Use purchased potting soil blended with sand and peat.
- Crowd the strawberry plants, fanning out the roots in slits as described above in "Planting Methods."

SUPPORT: None needed.

ONGOING CARE:
- **Removing blossoms:** If you are planting Junebearing strawberries, remove all blossoms the first year.

    If you choose everbearing or day-neutral strawberries, remove the blossoms until the Fourth of July. Then allow the plants to set fruit, and you'll be eating strawberries by August. This assumes you planted your strawberries in early spring. If you planted them in late spring or early summer, keep removing the blossoms until August.
- **Weeding:** Strawberries can be a challenge:
    —Hoeing can damage the shallow roots, and you can accidentally dig out strawberry plants.
    —Tilling works well between strawberry rows and is great for removing the old stock, but the tiller can't be used on weeds in the spaces between the daughters.
    —Hand pulling is tedious and time-consuming. (If you must hand weed, use a small campstool. When you've pulled all the weeds within reach, move the stool to the next spot.)

    Good news! There is a weeding solution that is easy and works quite well—an all-natural powder named Wow! available from Gardens Alive! (see "Sources"). You broadcast it all over the strawberry bed in very early spring, before the weeds have started, and again in the fall. The product is made in Iowa from corn, and it prevents seed from germinating. It won't stop weeds that are already growing, however—you'll still have to pull these—so be sure to get the Wow! on your strawberries early.

- **Frost Protection:** In the spring or the fall, established strawberry plants can tolerate a frost, but the blossoms might be damaged, particularly the sex organs that produce pollen. When you find berries that are tiny or malformed, it's possibly from poor pollination, due to frost damage.

  The first berries of the season are always the largest, so you don't want to risk them. If the strawberries are starting to bloom and frost is forecast, just spread some loose straw or an old blanket or sheet over the bed. Be sure to remove it in the early morning sun the next day.

  NOTE: Short, cool days stimulate flower growth, and long, hot days stimulate runner growth.

PRUNING: None, except for removing all runners to allow the plants to become established the first season.

POLLINATION: Strawberries are self-pollinating and the berries will be ready to eat about one month later.

WINTER PROTECTION:

- **From weather:** If you live in a severely cold climate and you have a constant blanket of snow on your strawberry patch all winter, they'll overwinter just fine. But if you have severe cold without the snow, you'll need to protect the strawberries with three or four inches of straw or mulch. If the layer is too thick or dense, the plants will smother, so be sure the protection is loose to allow for aeration.

  Put the cover in place only after you've had two or three hard frosts and the ground has frozen, and be sure to take it off in very early spring, perhaps leaving about one inch of loose straw over the crowns. The leaves will grow through it and you'll have an extra measure of protection.

If you live in an area that receives lots of rainfall over winter, do not apply mulch to the strawberries. The mulch will hold in water and make the strawberry crowns rot.

- **From varmints:** Be sure to use the grocery bag or other repellent method. One year, deer and rabbits destroyed one of my well-established strawberry beds when they were short on food.

PROPAGATION: The plants reproduce by sending out runners, or shoots about one or two feet long, that have tiny little strawberry plants at the end. When these baby plants come into contact with soil, they root and are called "daughters." The connecting arm is much like an umbilical cord, allowing the young plants to draw nutrients and water from the mother plant—and, if necessary, the mother plant can draw nutrients and water from the rooted daughter plants, as well.

About one month after touching soil, the daughter plants can be cut off the mother plant, dug, and transplanted.

If you use one of the planting methods that requires removing the daughters, be sure to take the entire runner. If you leave the arm, the node with tiny leaves located further up the runner arm will develop a new daughter.

VARIETIES INCLUDE: NOTE: Before purchasing your strawberry plants, be sure to read about the varieties available in nursery catalogues or check with your local supplier for recommendations for your area.

Junebearing:

- **Honeoye,** which is known for outstanding flavor. The honey-sweet, juicy, and firm berries are shaped like cones. Good fresh or cooked. Zones 3–8.
- **Dunlap,** an old variety that is drought-resistant and will grow anywhere if it is mulched. Firm, flavorful berries. Zones 4–8.
- **Big Boy,** which produces huge wedge-shaped berries that are up to two and a half inches across and sugar-sweet.

Everbearing:

- **Fort Laramie,** which yields heavily, yet tolerates cold and heat. Zones 4–8.
- **Ogallala,** which tolerates cold weather and drought and still bears a nice crop of sweet berries. Prolific and winter-hardy. Zones 3–8.
- **Sweet Charlie** is a good choice for the South because it is tolerant of heat and humidity yet produces flavorful berries. Zones 7–9.

Day-Neutral:

- **All Summer Long**, which produces high yields of medium-sized berries as the name implies, all summer long.
- **Tristar** produces large fruit that are great eaten fresh or frozen. Zones 4–8.
- **Selva** strawberries bear very large fruit with exceptional flavor. Good fresh, frozen, or cooked. Zones 5–9.
- **Ozark Beauty**, a popular strawberry that bears lots of large, juicy, sugar-sweet berries excellent fresh, frozen, or cooked. Zones 4–8.

FRUITING: You will have strawberries the first season if you've planted the day-neutral varieties and removed all blossoms and runners until July. Other types should not be allowed to fruit until their second year.

YIELD: Once established, each strawberry plant can yield a quart of fruit over a season.

HARVESTING: Strawberries will not ripen after they are picked, so don't harvest them until they are solid red, with no white or green, and the berries are firm and plump. Avoid harvesting the strawberries when the plants are wet.

Pick the strawberry by pinching the stem between the berry and the plant—don't pull on the berry itself.

Strawberries in the Kitchen

Leave the green caps intact until you are ready to eat the strawberries, because the berries will keep better and retain their vitamin C.

Refrigerate the strawberries without first washing them. As with other berries, line the container with a paper towel or terry-cloth towel and cover the fruit with the same material—never use plastic wrap or place strawberries in a sealed plastic container, which makes the berries spoil quickly in the refrigerator.

To wash strawberries, place the fruit in a colander and rinse with cold water. Do not hull the berries (remove the green caps) before you rinse them because they will bleed and you'll lose the flavorful fruit juice. Do not soak the berries or they might become soggy.

Don't keep fresh homegrown strawberries too long, because they deteriorate much quicker than the store-bought varieties. If you can't eat them fresh, cook or freeze them right away, or give them to a lucky friend!

Freezing Strawberries

DRY PACK: Rinse the berries and pat dry. Hull the berries. If they are bleeding, place them directly in containers or plastic bags. If they aren't bleeding much, you can lay them in a single layer on a baking sheet and collect them into a freezer bag or freezer container after they're frozen. The latter method is easier when you decide to use the frozen fruit, because it will be loose, whereas the bleeding fruit will tend to freeze into a block.

SUGAR PACK: Some people like to freeze strawberries with sugar, using 1 part sugar per 6 parts halved or sliced strawberries.

OTHER: Strawberries freeze well cooked into sauce or butter, or baked into pies.

Eating Strawberries

Everyone knows how delightful strawberries are when eaten fresh—in fact, when strawberries are picked, many don't make it to the house. The Farmer says that's the price of harvest!

Strawberries freeze well and are wonderful cooked.

Serving Ideas

- Strawberries can be served whole topped with a dollop of whipped cream or sliced and drizzled with milk or cream and perhaps a sprinkle of sugar.
- To dress them up a bit, layer strawberries in parfait glasses with ice cream or whipped cream or perhaps torn up pieces of white or yellow cake. Top with a dollop of whipped cream and a whole strawberry, perhaps garnished with a fresh mint leaf. Fast and easy!
- For a quick salad, strawberries can be folded into mayonnaise, whipped cream, or yogurt.
- Combine a little honey, lemon juice, and cognac. Pour over strawberries and chill for an easy salad.
- Toss strawberries with orange or grapefruit segments and banana slices.
- Toss sliced strawberries with crushed pineapple and perhaps banana slices.
- Combine sliced strawberries and diced orange segments.

Strawberry Ice Cream: Five Ways

1. Puree rinsed, patted dry, and hulled strawberries in a food processor to make 2 cups.
2. Add the following to the puree and blend in the food processor:

   1/3 cup sugar

   2 cups heavy whipping cream, half-and-half, buttermilk, or combination of these (NOTE: You can substitute 2 cups of plain vanilla yogurt, if desired.)

   1 tablespoon lemon juice

3. Add *one* of the following for flavoring:

> 1 teaspoon real vanilla extract
> 1/2 teaspoon almond extract
> 2 tablespoons crème de cacao
> 3 tablespoons amaretto
> 2 tablespoons triple sec orange liqueur

4. Place the mixture into your ice-cream maker and follow the manufacturer's instructions.

Strawberry Ice

1. Puree rinsed, patted dry, and hulled strawberries in a food processor to make 2 cups.
2. Mix in:

> 1/2 cup sugar
> 1/3 cup lemon juice or orange juice or combination
> 1/2 cup water

3. Place the mixture in your ice cream maker and follow the manufacturer's instructions.

Strawberry Sauce

This is one fruit sauce that's not cooked!

Clean and hull fresh strawberries and place in a bowl. With a potato masher, gently crush the berries to stimulate the juice. Sprinkle lightly with sugar, if desired, to bring out even more juice. Chill and serve.

For a variation, you can slice some ripe bananas into the strawberry sauce. The flavors go together wonderfully well!

Strawberry-Rhubarb Sauce

1. Combine in a saucepan:

> 2 cups cleaned, hulled, and sliced strawberries
> 2 cups sliced rhubarb
> 1/2 to 1 cup sugar

2. Simmer together just until fruit is tender. Serve hot or cold.

Strawberry Butter: Two Ways

1. In a saucepan, combine:

> 4 cups strawberry puree
> ⅔ cup sugar

2. Cook on high heat, stirring constantly. Begin timing when mixture comes to a boil. Boil 3 minutes, stirring constantly, on high heat. Remove from heat.
3. Stir in flavoring of choice:

> 2 tablespoons brandy plus ½ teaspoon cinnamon
>> or
> 1 tablespoon triple sec orange liqueur plus 1 tablespoon lemon juice

4. Serve warm or cold or place in containers and freeze.

Old-Fashioned Strawberry Pie

1. Place about 6 cups hulled strawberries in an unbaked pie shell. Large strawberries can be cut in half.
2. Combine ¾ cup sugar with ½ cup flour and pour over the strawberries.
3. Sprinkle generously with cinnamon (optional) and dot liberally with butter.
4. Top with crust and seal. Prick crust with the tip of a paring knife in several places for ventilation. Sprinkle crust lightly with sugar, if desired.
5. Bake at 425 degrees F for 40 minutes or until crust is golden brown. Serve warm or cold, plain or with whipped cream or ice cream.

Glazed Strawberry Pie

1. Remove 4 ounces of cream cheese from the refrigerator; allow to come to room temperature.
2. Prepare a pie shell, prick it all over with a fork, and bake it till lightly browned. Cool.

3. In a small saucepan, simmer about 3 minutes:

> I cup strawberries, crushed with a fork.
> ½ cup water

4. In a small bowl, combine

> I cup sugar
> 3 tablespoons corn starch
> ½ cup cool water

5. Add the sugar mixture to the saucepan and stir together. Bring to boiling and boil 1 minute, stirring constantly. Remove from heat.
6. Spread the cream cheese on the bottom of the pie shell. Arrange about 4 cups of fresh, whole strawberries on top of the cream cheese. Pour the glaze over the strawberries and chill for about 2 hours before serving. If desired, top with dollops of whipped cream—wonderful!

Chocolate-Covered Strawberries

So pretty—and delicious!

First wash the strawberries, and be certain they are completely dry. Leave the green leafy caps on the stem end. Place ½ cup semisweet real chocolate or white chocolate morsels with 1½ teaspoons butter in a microwave-safe glass measuring cup. Do not cover chocolate. Microwave on the high setting for 10 seconds; stir and repeat until chocolate is barely melted. Hold the strawberries by their caps and dip in the chocolate so that half the red is covered. Place on waxed paper until the chocolate is set.

WATERMELON IN THE GARDEN

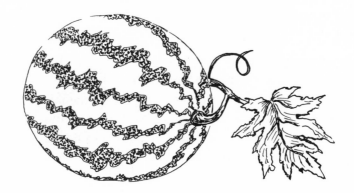

Ah, watermelon! It conjures up Fourth-of-July images of oblong snake-striped fruit chilling in icy water tanks before being cut into thick half-circle slabs so sweet and succulent you want to bury your face in the bright red flesh. As with most other fruits, the best melons are picked ripe from your own garden and are far superior to those picked slightly green for shipping. The sugar is manufactured in those final days of ripening, and that's what is missing in store-bought watermelon.

The fruit can have skins that are light green, dark green, or both light and dark green in zigzag stripes. We think of watermelon flesh as being a bright pinkish red, but it can also be orange, yellow, or white, depending on the variety and the ripeness. The fruit can be large or small; round, oblong, or cylindrical.

Typically, watermelons are full of black seeds. Now there are seedless varieties available, which actually do have tiny white undeveloped seeds that are soft and can be eaten with the flesh.

Description

Watermelon is an annual vining plant that is related to cucumbers, squash, pumpkins, and other melons.

As a vine, watermelon can take up lots of space; however, there are compact varieties available. Or, watermelon can be grown on a strong support—be sure to have a very secure sling to cradle the heavy fruit, and tie up the vines with cloth or pantyhose, not wire.

LOCATION: The watermelon patch should be relocated every year, to discourage insect and disease problems. Don't plant watermelons where cucumbers, squash, pumpkins, or other melons grew the previous two years.

Farmers grow melons on a sandy slope or hill where other crops don't do well. The sandy slope not only accomplishes good drainage, but it is likely to have good air circulation, which is important to prevent disease. The downside is that watermelons on a sandy hill need regular watering or they won't produce; try to locate the patch near a water source.

Watermelon can cross-pollinate with other types of melon, but this doesn't affect this year's fruit, only the seeds. If you used these seeds the next year, you wouldn't get a true variety.

GROWING RANGE: Watermelons will grow anywhere with a warm growing season that is long enough to mature the melons on the vines. They love hot, sunny days and cooler nights. If you live in a short season area, consider planting the compact bush varieties, which ripen in much less time.

CHILL REQUIREMENT: None.

SOIL: Watermelons prefer sandy, well-drained soil with lots of moisture. They also need good nutrition; farmers till in about three inches of well-rotted manure over the planting area, but you can substitute compost.

MOISTURE: Water the plants profusely every week if you don't get sufficient rain. Watermelons need lots of water, although they do not like soggy roots. To prevent disease, direct the water to the roots, not the vines, or else water early in the morning so that the vines will dry quickly in the sun.

If you live in an area with lots of rain, till sand into the soil before planting, or else use raised planters. If you live in a dry area, consider burying a one-gallon plastic milk jug that has been perforated with a nail, in the soil so that the top two inches remain above the ground. Then plant the watermelon seeds in a cluster around the buried jug. To water, just fill the buried jug, using a hose or watering can.

LIGHT: Full sun.

PLANTING SEASON: Spring, after all danger of frost.

HOW TO PLANT: Watermelons must be started each year from seed.

- Start planting seeds one week before the last frost date for your area, or when the soil temperature is at least 65 degrees F, or the seed won't germinate.
- Till the soil thoroughly, mixing in well-rotted manure or compost, and sand, if needed.
- If desired, put down landscaping cloth to warm the soil for one or two weeks before planting, and cut an X in the cloth to plant the seeds.
- If desired, bury a plastic milk jug as described in "Moisture," above.
- Plant watermelons together in a cluster called a hill, placing two or three seeds four to six inches apart, forming a triangle. Cover the seeds with one inch of soil.
- Space the hills for compact bush types three of four feet apart in rows six or eight feet apart; space the larger vining types up to ten feet apart in all directions.

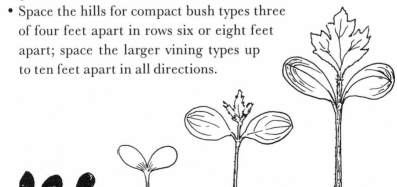

- Keep the seeds evenly moist and they'll germinate in about one week.
- You can cover the seed clusters with plastic one-gallon milk jugs that have had the bottom cut out—this will help maintain soil warmth, which will assist germination and protect the seedlings. Anchor the milk cartons securely in the ground. Remove the cap for ventilation as soon as the seeds have germinated, to prevent moisture buildup inside the milk jugs, which can cause disease.

To start your own seedlings: It's best to direct-plant the seeds outside, but you can start them indoors about two weeks before transplanting time. Use peat pots because the roots are very sensitive to any disturbance. Transplant the seedlings one or two weeks after the last frost date.

NOTE: If the soil isn't warm enough before you plant the seeds or transplant the seedlings, you risk not only nongermination, but the plants may later be unable to set fruit.

SUPPORT: None required.

ONGOING CARE: When the seedlings are up, you can thin them back to two plants per hill or just one plant, if you have a short summer or your soil is poor.

FERTILIZING: If you don't have rotted manure for fertilizer, seaweed emulsion is great. Apply it according to directions at planting, at fruit set, and two weeks after fruit set.

If you didn't use landscaping cloth, you should cover the ground with a thick mulch—but don't do this until the seedlings are well up and the soil is warm. If possible, this is best done after a good rain. Mulch will keep the vines, and especially the fruit, off the damp soil, preventing disease and insect problems.

After the melons are evident, I like to place cement slabs, a scrap board, or some other support under each fruit to raise it above any moisture, even when using mulch.

When walking in the watermelon patch, be careful that you don't step on any of the delicate vines. If the vines grow outside their designated area, gently redirect them.

In late summer, remove all the blossoms so that the vines concentrate their energy on the existing fruit. Also, remove the smallest fruit so that the remaining watermelons can develop. The watermelons won't be as large as those growing all summer, but the later-developing watermelons can be tasty, because the plant senses that the days are shorter, and it rushes to develop the fruit to maturity at a smaller size.

PRUNING: None needed.

POLLINATION: Watermelon can be self-pollinating, but most are helped by bees.

The seedless varieties need a pollinator, and seed companies include seeds for the pollinator in the seed packet.

WINTER PROTECTION: None, the plants don't survive in winter.

PROPAGATION: Seeds.

VARIETIES INCLUDE:
- **Extra Early Sugar Baby** is a great choice if space is limited, because it's suited for a trellis. The perfectly round fruit is six or seven inches in diameter and has a dark-green skin and crisp, deep red flesh with few seeds. Ready in 80 days.
- **Crimson Sweet** has vigorous vines that produce fifteen- to twenty-five-pound blocky-round fruit. The skins are thin and striped; the flesh is bright red and fine in texture and very sweet. The seeds are half the size of regular watermelons'.
- **Carolina Cross #183** is the one to choose if you want to raise watermelons that weigh up to two hundred pounds. The melons are oblong and striped, and the flesh is bright red, sweet, and juicy. Ready in 95 days.
- **Golden Crown Hybrid** bears oblong five- to seven-pound fruit with skin that turns golden yellow when the fruit is ripe. The flesh remains red and is sweet. Ready in 78 days.

- **Yellow Doll Hybrid** has rounded six- to eight-pound fruit with green-striped skin, but the flesh is bright yellow, very sweet, and delicious. A good choice for trellising. Ready in 65 days.
- **King of Hearts** is a seedless variety that bears blocky-oblong fruit weighing fourteen to eighteen pounds with striped skins and bright red flesh that's firm and crisp.

FRUITING: Smaller bush-type watermelons can be harvested in about 70 days; larger vine-types can be harvested about 100 to 120 days after planting.

YIELD: Smaller bush-type plants produce up to ten melons weighing three or four pounds each; larger vines produce two or three melons weighing anywhere from ten to over a hundred pounds each.

HARVESTING: As Mark Twain once said, when you thump a watermelon and the sound you hear is "pink" or "pank," leave it because it's not ripe enough until you hear "punk."

The tendril closest to the fruit stem will look dead and the stems will look brittle when the watermelon is ripe. If the stem breaks off easily when you pick up the watermelon, it's ready. On some varieties, the whitish skin on the underside turns yellow when the watermelon is ripe; if the underside is white or pale green, the watermelon is not ripe.

Watermelon in the Kitchen

If you've eaten part of a watermelon, just cover the cut surface with plastic wrap and store the rest in the refrigerator. Or remove the flesh from the rind, cut it into chunks, and place the chunks in covered plastic containers in the refrigerator.

To remove the seeds from a watermelon, cut it in half and then in quarters, the long way, through the stem. Then cut through the melon along the seed line and lift off the top wedge, which is seed-free. Use a meat fork to scrape off the seeds and then the remaining flesh attached to the rind will be seed-free.

Freezing Watermelon

DRY PACK:
- Remove the seeds and peel and slice the watermelon into one-inch cubes.
- Some people think watermelon freezes better if you sprinkle the chunks with lemon juice (optional).
- Pack the watermelon into freezer containers. Seal, label, and freeze.

Serve when only partially thawed, or else make it into ice cream or ice.

Eating Watermelon

A well-chilled watermelon just can't be beat on a hot summer day! Serve it on large plates with forks to pick out the seeds; or let everyone eat it outside where they can simply spit the seeds on the ground!

Serving Ideas

- Watermelon chunks or balls make a great addition to fruit salads.

245

- Watermelon can be pureed (minus the rind and seeds) and served, chilled, as a fruit juice.
- Freeze the pureed watermelon or the watermelon juice in an ice cube tray; add the frozen cubes to fruit drinks.
- Combine watermelon chunks with pineapple for a quick salad.
- For a buffet-type meal, you can cut a watermelon into a basket shape, leaving a strip for the "handle." Scoop out the flesh with a melon baller. Decorate the watermelon basket by cutting "teeth" edges, or cover the white rind with a row of fruits, like grapes and strawberries, attached with toothpicks. If the basket won't sit level, trim off a little rind from the bottom. Fill with a fruit blend, perhaps adding strawberries, cantaloupe, peaches, blueberries, and grapes to the watermelon balls. Add a serving spoon, and this will be a popular attraction!

Easy Watermelon Ice Cream

Excellent—perfect for a hot summer night!

1. Cut the watermelon flesh free from the rind and remove the seeds, or use a seedless variety. Puree the watermelon to make 2 cups.
2. Blend in:

   1/2 teaspoon lemon juice
   1/4 to 1/2 cup sugar
   1 cup heavy cream

3. Place the mixture in your ice-cream maker and follow the manufacturer's instructions. Serve sprinkled with a little ground nutmeg or chopped fresh (best) or dried mint, if desired.

Easy Watermelon Ice

1. Remove rind and seeds and cut watermelon into chunks. Puree chunks in a food processor to make 4 cups.
2. Add ¼ to ½ cup sugar and ¼ cup lemon juice and blend well. If desired, add 2 tablespoons of brandy.
3. Pour the mixture into your ice-cream maker and follow manufacturer's instructions. Or, if you don't have an ice-cream maker, put the mixture in your freezer in a large metal bowl; remove it after 15 minutes and beat well. Repeat this several times until firm enough to serve.

Watermelon-Onion Salad

I first had this unusual dish at a friend's house.
1. Remove rind and cut watermelon into bite-sized chunks to make 4 cups. If desired, remove seeds and make watermelon balls instead.
2. Toss together with:
> ½ cup quartered and thinly sliced sweet onion
> ¼ cup chopped fresh basil
> ¼ cup raspberry vinegar
> salt and pepper (optional)

3. Serve chilled on a bed of lettuce.

Watermelon "Cake"

A light and easy summer dessert!
1. Cut a 3- or 4-inch slice from the center of a chilled watermelon. Lay this slice flat. Cut vertical slits through the rind in several places and carefully trim off the rind in sections. Place the watermelon slice on a cake plate and blot the surface with paper towels to absorb the juice.
2. In a mixing bowl, whip 1½ cups heavy cream plus 1 tablespoon powdered milk.
3. Blend in one 8-ounce carton of lemon yogurt.

4. Frost the top and sides of the watermelon with the whipped lemon cream.

5. Refrigerate until chilled and serve, but do not hold the "cake" longer than 5 or 6 hours. Serve like cake by slicing wedges.

NOTE: For convenience, you might select a seedless watermelon variety for this recipe, or else people can pick out the seeds with their forks.

Watermelon Pie

1. Whip together 1½ cups heavy cream and 2 tablespoons powdered milk.

2. Stir in one 3-ounce package of watermelon-flavored gelatin.

3. Fold in 3 cups watermelon cubes, with the seeds removed (or use a seedless watermelon variety).

4. Pour watermelon filling into a graham cracker crust. Chill.

5. Serve very cold. If your refrigerator isn't cold enough, chill the pie in the freezer until partially frozen, about 30 minutes, and serve partially frozen.

Watermelon Soup

1. Puree watermelon to make 3 cups.

2. Peel and slice a ½-inch slice of gingerroot that is 1 inch in diameter. Mince. Add a little of the watermelon puree to it and blend well, then add it to the rest of the watermelon.

3. Stir in:

> ¼ cup white wine
> 1 ½ tablespoons lemon juice
> 1 ½ tablespoons minced fresh mint leaves or use
>   ½ tablespoon dried mint
> 2 teaspoons sugar

4. Chill. Serve in small soup bowls or cups, garnished with a dollop of whipped cream and a fresh mint leaf, if desired.

SOURCES

Books

Fruit, Berry and Nut Inventory is an annual, comprehensive sourcebook for all fruits, berries, nuts, and tropical edibles available from U.S. mail-order nurseries. Includes contact information. A must have! (You also might want to consider joining their fine organization or visiting their test gardens.) The book is available from:

> Seed Savers Exchange
> 3076 North Winn Road
> Decorah, IA 52101
> www.seedsavers.org

Machinery and Tools

Mantis Tiller is the very best portable tiller on the market. Their claims are not exaggerated. If you don't agree, you can return it within one year for a full refund. Call 1-800-366-6268 for free information or check their Web site, where you can also find composters, sprayers, and other useful equipment:

> www.mantistiller.com

Gardener's Supply Company has great equipment and tools for the gardener.

> Gardener's Supply Company
> 128 Intervale Road
> Burlington, VT 05401
> 800-427-3363
> www.gardeners.com

Garden Tools by Lee Valley also has excellent equipment and tools for the gardener.

> 12 East River Street
> Ogdensburg, NY 13669
> www.leevalley.com

Harris Seeds Home Gardening Catalogue has top quality light stands and other seed starting equipment and supplies.

> 355 Paul Road/P.O. Box 24966
> Rochester, NY 14624-0966
> 800-514-4441
> www.harrisseeds.com

Cuisinart makes wonderful time-saving food processors, cordless hand blenders, and electric ice cream makers, as well as quality stainless steel pots and pans. These products are available in stores and catalogues nationwide, or you can visit the Cuisinart Web site at:

> www.cuisinart.com

Organizations

The **Hobby Greenhouse Association** is worth joining, even if you don't own a greenhouse!

> Hobby Greenhouse Association
> 8 Glen Terrace
> Bedford, MA 01730-2048
> www.hobbygreenhouse.org

The Seed Savers Exchange is a nonprofit organization dedicated to maintaining our plant diversity by saving heirloom fruit and vegetable varieties from extinction. You can visit their gardens on 18,000 acres near Decorah, Iowa, or attend informational gatherings. For more information, contact:

> Seed Savers Exchange
> 3076 North Winn Road
> Decorah, IA 52101
> www.seedsavers.org

4-H is a program for youth in cooperation with the Extension service. It originated in a small Iowa community and has become an international organization. For more information, contact:

> National 4-H Council
> 7100 Connecticut Avenue
> Chevy Chase, MD 20815
> 301-961-2800
> www.fourhcouncil.edu

Products

Gardens Alive! Environmentally Responsible Products That Work is a mail-order company that provides everything from all-natural fertilizers to fruit sprays and pest and disease controls. Their catalogue is well illustrated to help you identify your problem and tells how to implement the solution. I am very happy with the products from this company and recommend them highly. To get a catalogue:

> Gardens Alive!
> 5100 Schenley Place
> Lawrenceburg, IN 47025
> Customer Service: 812-537-8651, Mon. to Fri., 8 A.M. to 5 P.M., E.T.
> www.GardensAlive.com

NURSERIES AND MAIL-ORDER CATALOGUES FOR FRUITS AND BERRIES

W. Atlee Burpee and Co.
300 Park Avenue
Warminster, PA 18991
800-888-1447
Free catalogue, many fruit varieties, also has
    strawberry pyramid kit.
www.burpee.com

The Cook's Garden
P. O. Box 535
Londonderry, VT 05148
800-457-9703
www.cooksgarden.com

Edible Forest Nursery
P.O. Box 260195
Madison, WI 53726-0195
Free catalogue, cold-hardy fruit, zones 3—4.
Toll-free: 877-745-8267

Farmer Seed and Nursery Co.
818 NW 4th Street
Faribault, MN 55021
Free catalogue, many fruit varieties.

Forestfarm Nursery
990 Tetherow Road

Williams, OR 97544
Free catalog, many fruit varieties, affordable
    prices.
541-846-7269
www.forestfarm.com

Garden of Delights
14560 SW 14th Street
Davie, FL 33325-4217
Catalogue, $2, has tropical and subtropical fruits.
www.gardenofdelights.com

Gurney's Seed and Nursery Co.
P. O. Box 778
Yankton, SD 57079-0778
Free catalogue. "America's Most Complete
    Seed and Nursery Company."
812-539-2499
www.gurneys.com

Harris Seeds Home Gardening Catalogue
355 Paul Road/ P. O. Box 24966
Rochester, NY 14624-0966
800-514-4441
Free catalogue. "120 Years of Friendly and
    Courteous Service."
www.harrisseeds.com

Hartmann's Plantation, Inc.
P.O. Box 100
Lacota, MI 49063
Has blueberries, gooseberries, kiwis, rasp-
    berries, etc.
www.hartmannsplantcompany.com

Henry Field's Seed and Nursery Co.
P.O. Box 600
Shenandoah, IA 51602-0001
Free catalogue, many fruit varieties, also has
    a strawberry pyramid kit.
812-539-2521
www.henryfields.com

Hidden Springs Nursery
170 Hidden Springs Lane
Cookeville, TN 38501
Catalogue, $1, includes mulberries, elder-
    berries, gooseberries, kiwis.
931-268-2592

Hilltop Nurseries
P.O. Box 578
Hartford, MI 49057
Many fruit trees, wholesale and retail.
616-621-3135

J.W. Jung Seed Co.
335 S. High Street
Randolph, WI 53957-0001
Free catalog. "Quality Seeds, Plants, Garden
    Gifts & Bulbs."
800-247-5864
www.jungseed.com

Kiwis "R" Us
5 Tippets Road
Nesquehoning, PA 18240
Specializes in hardy kiwis, offers 26 varieties.

Lee's Nursery
P. O. Box 489
McMinnville, TN 37111-0489
Free catalogue, many fruit varieties.
931-668-4870

Mellinger's Inc.
2310 South Range Road
North Lima, OH 44452
Free catalogue, many fruits and berries.
330-549-9861
www.mellingers.com

Miller Nurseries
5060 W. Lake Road
Canandaigua, NY 14424-8904
Free catalogue, specializes in fruiting plants.
800-836-9630
www.millernurseries.com

Park Seed Co.
1 Parkton Ave.
Greenwood, SC 29647-0001
Free catalogue.
800-845-3369
www.parkseed.com

Raintree Nursery
391 Butts Road
Morton, WA 98356
Free catalogue.
360-496-6400
www.raintreenursery.com

Seeds of Change: Goodness From the
    Ground Up
P.O. Box 15700
Santa Fe, NM 87592-1500
888-762-7333
www.seedsofchange.com

Shepherd's Garden Seeds
30 Irene Street
Torrington, CT 06790-6658
Free catalogue, has good fruit varieties.
860-482-3638
www.shepherdseeds.com

Sonoma Antique Apple Nursery
4395 Westside Road
Healdsburg, CA 95448
Free catalogue, has many fruits besides apples.
707-433-6420
www.applenursery.com

INDEX